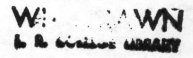

JOSE DE ESPRONCEDA

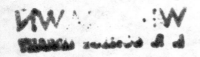

RICARDO LANDEIRA

JOSE DE ESPRONCEDA

SOCIETY OF SPANISH AND SPANISH-AMERICAN STUDIES

THE SOCIETY OF SPANISH AND SPANISH-AMERICAN STUDIES PROMOTES BIBLIOGRAPHICAL, CRITICAL AND PEDAGOGICAL RESEARCH IN SPANISH AND SPANISH-AMERICAN STUDIES BY PUBLISHING WORKS OF PARTICULAR MERIT IN THESE AREAS. ON OCCASION, THE SOCIETY WILL ALSO PUBLISH CREATIVE WORKS. SSSAS IS A NON-PROFIT EDUCATIONAL ORGANIZATION SPONSORED BY THE UNIVERSITY OF NEBRASKA-LINCOLN. IT IS LOCATED AT THE DEPARTMENT OF MODERN LANGUAGES AND LITERATURES. THE UNIVERSITY OF NEBRASKA-LINCOLN, OLDFATHER HALL, LINCOLN, NEBRASKA 68588-0316, U.S.A.

Library of Congress Catalog Card Number: 84-050239
ISBN: 0-89295-032-3

SSSAS: LC-1946

For Joy

CONTENTS

PREFACE

José de Espronceda does not want for lack of critical attention. His bibliography ranks among the longest in nineteenth century peninsular Spanish literature and yet most items in this list which includes thousands of entries are hopelessly inadequate or misleading. Until the very recent work of scholars such as Angel Antón Andrés, David J. Billick, Joaquín Casalduero and Robert Marrast (see BIBLIOGRAPHY), among a few, Espronceda has been portrayed invariably as an *enfant terrible* adopting the pose of a Spanish Lord Byron, egocentric, thoughtless and unoriginal who could devote little time and less constancy even to his best mistress, Literature.

Incredibly, one hundred and thirty years passed before a rigorous critical edition of Espronceda's collection of poems, *Poesías,* first issued in 1840, was published. His novel *Sancho Saldaña* (1834) finally received such attention in 1974. The only short story to come from his pen, «La pata de palo,» as of this writing, has been analyzed in print on a single occasion. In terms of other critical scrutinies and reliable editions only *El Estudiante de Salamanca* and *El Diablo Mundo* have fared better. The bulk of studies dedicated to either the man or his works brim with *idées reçues* that have gone unrevised for decades, or else they have been written by sycophants. To this date no complete works edition exists and, perhaps less surprising, there is no book-length study in English on the subject.

Espronceda is the most important poet in Spanish literature during the century and a half following the deaths of Góngora and Quevedo. As a Romantic, he towers above his contemporaries and above those who, as post-Romantics, were to come after him, not only as a poet but also as the most representative figure of his age. Of the two men against whom José de Espronceda is most often measured, José Zorrilla and Gustavo Adolfo Bécquer, neither was accosted by the deep sense of disillusionment that preyed upon him most of his life. Zorrilla was not as concerned with the present as with a past that he conceived as legendary, Catholic and replete with chivalric adventure. Bécquer, burdened by sickness, indigence and

familial unhappiness, sought refuge in a fantasy world of his own imagining. Reality as such never punctured their escapist—though
diverse—microcosms, whereas in Espronceda's verse as well as in his prose,
reality intruded inescapably.

Aesthetic distance in Espronceda's poetry is never too significant,
which is not to say that all of his poems grow out of a real circumstance,
nor that all of those which do are uniformly memorable. Yet, among his
most important compositions, those deriving from daily life or the poet's
own experience, having an ascendancy other than a strictly literary one, are
truly masterpieces. In the totality of Espronceda's production, above all in
his lyric verse, its two fundamental leitmotifs—the sentimental and the
socio-political—reflect the poet's increasing pessimism with the passing of
the years. This trajectory of bitterness suggests an increasing realization of
the chasm separating what Espronceda, as a poet, imagined and what, as a
man, he could reach. He was confronted with a basic incongruence between ideological desirability and vital posture, hence the ascending index
of *angst* and rebellion. A consciousness of this disproportion between the
imaginable and the attainable led Espronceda to despair, initially, because
he felt incapable of bridging the distance that separates them and, subsequently, because he could not adjust his desires to the possibilities that lay
before him.

Espronceda the ideologue, defender of individual liberty and of
equality among men, is the common persona between the poet and the
political activist. That he managed to succeed in both dimensions,
graduating from neoclassical apprentice to the foremost romantic, and
from an adolescent conspirator to a mature member of the *Cortes*,
represents a considerable achievement.

It is because I believed that the Espronceda phenomenon had to be
reappraised from a more dispassionate and fresh perspective that I under-
took the writing of this monograph. The new critical editions now being
made available by some of the scholars cited above have been invaluable
for such a task. Equally helpful was a thorough study of the original texts
themselves and a willingness to arrive at interpretations that at times did
not correspond with the traditional ones perpetuated through the years and
accepted as irrefutable. In endeavoring to revise the portrayal of those who
have, in my opinion, misjudged him, this is the José de Espronceda I have
found through the analysis of his works and the reading of his brief thirty-
four year biography: A most accomplished man of letters and a serious,
selfless and responsible political activist guided in both disciplines by a
desire to secure individual freedom and equality for all.

As a result of the already-noted lack of a book-length study in English

on Espronceda or his writings, I have examined, within the given space con-
strictions, the greatest portion of the poet's works. Individual chapters
devoted to his biography, his most important poems, his theater, his prose,
as well as an introductory one on Spanish Romanticism make up the bulk
of this slim volume. Its purpose, then, is to offer the general reader of
Spanish literature as comprehensive a look as possible into Spain's most
consummate and least outmoded Romantic.

RICARDO LANDEIRA

University of Wyoming, 1984

CHAPTER ONE

The Romantic Life of José de Espronceda

In the early dawn of March 25, 1808, a cavalry unit of the Bourbon regiment, under the command of Lt. Colonel Juan Espronceda, made its way toward the city of Badajoz. Accompanying the chief officer was his wife, María del Carmen Delgado y Lara, who followed the troops in a horse-drawn carriage. Very much pregnant, though obliged to follow her husband in his transfer from their home in Villafranca de los Barros due to the nation's state of war with Napoleonic France, three-and-a-half miles from the town of Almendralejo in a place called Pajares de la Vega, Carmen gave birth to a boy at six-thirty in the morning. The mother, once comfortably installed for a rest at the palace of the Marquis of Monsalud, had the newborn infant christened at the church of Our Lady of Purification in Almendralejo with the names José Ignacio Javier. History knows him as José de Espronceda.

I. The Early Years

At the time of the child's birth Don Juan was nearing his fifty-ninth year and his wife her thirty-second. Apart from his advanced age as a father, Colonel Espronceda had a war of independence to fight against the French (1808-1814) which in his case meant being ordered to stand in Andalucía, Extremadura, La Coruña, Madrid and Guadalajara, among other fronts. Consequently, the task of rearing the son fell entirely on the mother, a strict disciplinarian who countered her husband's gentle and carefree domestic attitude toward the boy whenever on leave from the battlefield.

13

Home for the Esproncedas appears to have been Madrid during the years of fighting. Not far from Lobo street (renamed Echegaray in 1888) where the family lived, there opened in 1821 a private school, the Colegio de San Mateo, under the direction of the priest Juan Manuel Calleja who employed as teachers José Gómez Hermosilla and Alberto Lista. The latter, a remarkably enlightened educator and well-considered poet in his day, turned out to be the true spiritual leader of this small institution. It was under his tutelage that the young Espronceda, having declined an opening made for him at Segovia's Military Academy in July 1820, began his formal education at age thirteen. The program of studies must have been rather difficult for José, accustomed as he was to days filled largely with leisurely pranks and picaresque pastimes. The humanities played the larger role in Lista's classes and, within this framework, literature, mythology, languages and history filled most of the students' time. Not surprisingly José's main failing, as noted in his school records, lay in a lack of self-discipline and an aversion to the sciences. The school's reputation as the best of its kind in Madrid at that time, however, is evidenced by the progress slowly noted in Espronceda's studies. True, he was permitted to develop in the direction of his natural inclination which was poetic composition. Nevertheless, his training in this field of his choice was no less arduous or thorough. He became familiar with the Italians Torcuato Tasso and Ludovico Ariosto, with the writings of Voltaire, with Milton and Ossian, Homer, Virgil and other classics, Spanish ones included, through many readings, text analyses and his own imitations of their verse.

At the age of fifteen, Espronceda embarked upon a second and parallel course to his literary apprenticeship, one which lasted until his death—politics. The Madrid uprising of July 7, 1823, quashed in short order, inspired Espronceda's first poem entitled «Al 7 de julio,» which though lost seems to have merited Lista's approval. It pointed to Espronceda's penchant for transubstantiating political circumstance into verse form.

Soon after the tyrant Fernando VII had regained power, there began in Spain a long decade of reprisals and an iron-fisted rule that included the revival of the loathed Inquisition on the one hand and the closing of the nation's universities and schools on the other. Among the first to feel the ire of the despot was the brave General Riego, publicly hanged at the Plaza de la Cebada on November 7, 1823 for his support of the constitutional movement in opposition to the absolutist monarchy. In the mob witnessing the execution was Espronceda, together with a dozen or so of his friends who included the future poet Ventura de la Vega and his own earliest biographer, Patricio de la Escosura. At the conclusion of the gruesome spectacle, Espronceda and his cohorts adjourned to their drugstore-basement hide-out on Hortaleza Street to found a secret society called «Los Numantinos» and swore to avenge the death of their liberal hero, an oath taken down on paper and subsequently signed with their blood. Named after the besieged inhabitants of the ancient city of Numancia who died to the last citizen rather than surrender to the Roman legions, this society had no less a goal than to overthrow and punish the absolutist and capricious monarchy of Fernando VII. The paranoid character of Fernando's minions in wanting to stamp out all opposition was so extreme that when the «Numantino's» plot was uncovered and their extravagant document read, the young lot of them was condemned to long prison terms. Espronceda himself received a sentence of five years to be served at a Franciscan convent in Guadalajara, a city where his father was then stationed; no doubt a factor in the judges' decision. The guardian friar, obviously unimpressed with the teenager's crime, saw fit to certify that Espronceda had fulfilled his time of punishment only a few weeks after he had entered the monastery.

With the ban on schools in 1823 had come the demise of the Colegio de San Mateo but Alberto Lista agreed to continue teaching at his home on Valverde Street for a select group of his former pupils, among them Espronceda. The budding poet, meanwhile, with Lista's blessing, contributed to the founding of a literary club named the «Academia del Mirto» on April 24, 1823. Its activities consisted of giving free poetic rein to all the aspiring young members who joined, though their excesses must have been tempered by the constant presence of Lista who probably considered the «Academia del Mirto» an extension of his own more formal teachings. For the most part, the poetic exercises done here were of a classical cut, imitations or translations of Homer, Ovid, or modelled after equally classical Spanish traditionalists such as Fray Luis de León and Fernando de Herrera. Espronceda's earliest efforts fall within this same unoriginal category. «La tormenta en la noche,» «Romance a la mañana,» «La vida en el campo,» «La Noche,» «Vaticinio de Nereo,» and «A Anfriso en sus días,» all dating from his association days (1823-1826) with the «Academia,» betray a reverence for the traditional stanzas such as the ode, the ballad and the sonnet, and openly emulate the poetics of Homer as well as Herrera the way Lista had insisted his pupils learn to use them.

During his few months of confinement at the Franciscan monastery in Guadalajara, Espronceda had not been idle. In concert with his teacher Lista, an ambitious plan for an epic poem, «El Pelayo,» was drawn up. Dealing with the Spaniards' reconquest of their country from the Moors, the epic, written in formal *octavas reales* was never finished though

Espronceda may have intended to work on it toward the end of 1829. Lista himself contributed no less than sixty-one stanzas out of a total of one hundred and thirty.

II. Exile from Spain (1827-1833)

There can be little doubt that Espronceda, in spite of his father's influence as a loyal military man in the service of Fernando VII, was kept under surveillance on account of his many political and conspiratorial activities, however inconsequential these may have been. Such constricting measures together with a thirst for adventure which had emancipated him early on from his parents' authority contributed to the decision to leave Spain for neighboring Portugal. The biographical essay «De Gibraltar a Lisboa. Viaje histórico» detailed good-humoredly, some fourteen years after the event, the clandestine crossing between the southern English port and the Portuguese capital at the mouth of the Tagus river. Espronceda's name first appeared on the Lisbon police blotter on August 14, 1827, as a result of a directive to have him expelled from the country. His stay in Portugal was not as pleasant as he perhaps had anticipated. The Portuguese government looked upon political emigrés as undesirables to be put under lock and key. Espronceda soon found himself at the Santarem jail, penniless and with no one to turn to for help.

But not all was dark. Here in Lisbon and while in prison Espronceda would meet Teresa, the woman who for ten years filled his existence and inspired a significant portion of his writing. It remains unclear whether he met her father, Colonel Epifanio Mancha, a veteran political instigator and rebel, at Santarem or at the fortress of the San Jorge prison. Equally unresolved among Espronceda biographers are the circumstances of his first encounter with this beautiful Andalusian girl. Most evidence, however, points to their meeting as a result of her father's and Espronceda's friendship in whichever of the two places they both happened to be incarcerated. Teresa, a most attractive seventeen-year-old, was immediately drawn to the impetuous young Spaniard, and an affair ensued. Unfortunately, Espronceda was then deported from Portugal, choosing to go to England where he arrived on September 15, 1827.

In London's Summerstown district on 23 Bridge Water Street, the colony of Spanish exiles, Espronceda shared an apartment with Antonio Hernáiz, an ex-army lieutenant whom he had befriended in Lisbon. Wellington's Tory government looked kindly upon the Spanish exiles, who enjoyed as a result a monthly living allowance. Espronceda, aside from this pension which he may not have collected for very long according to the British treasury's official refugee pay lists,[1] derived an income from the fencing lessons he gave and from a regular allowance sent by his parents. Altogether, these sources represented a respectable amount of money, yet financial discipline like other types of responsibility was not Espronceda's concern since, in more than one instance, the letters addressed to his parents contain appeals for more money. The most notorious of these, written in early 1828, urged them to send enough *reales* to cover the amount owed his tailor. One dated November 18, 1828, mentioned the very real risk of going to jail if debts were not settled immediately.

Little else is known of what Espronceda did with his time while in London. He did not associate with the more famous liberal exiles such as Alcalá Galiano, Istúriz or Argüelles, nor did he wish to visit the Spanish Ambassador to Britain or any other friends of his parents due to their political ideas so contrary to his own. Strange as it may seem, none of the Spanish journals in London such as *El emigrado observador* or the *Ocios de españoles emigrados,* published at the time of Espronceda's residence in this city, carry articles of his. He did write several compositions, among them «La entrada del invierno en Londres» and «A la Patria,» both of which show an exile's love for his country and the pain felt at seeing it in the hands of a treacherous government. At this time Espronceda also asked his parents for the «Pelayo» manuscript that he wanted to show his friends in London and which he intended to complete while in idleness.

Having received enough money for the passage from his father Don Juan, on February 28, 1828, Espronceda journeyed to France reaching Belgium seven days later. Upon setting foot on the Continent, the Spanish authorities, who believed him to be a dangerous associate of the exiled guerrilla leader Mina, alerted the French police of his imminent arrival and urged them to keep Espronceda, together with his traveling companion, Lt. Hernáiz, well away from the Franco-Spanish border, fearing that the two emigrés intended to cross it and then would scheme to lead an insurrection in Navarra. That Espronceda's capacity for mayhem was not taken lightly can be ascertained from the house search carried out by suspicious police in Don Juan's Madrid residence looking for incriminating evidence against the young man. By mid-April, when Paris was beginning to feel the uneasiness resulting from the escalating confrontations between Charles X and the French Parliament, the two comrades were in the capital city living in the Favart Hotel. Espronceda's and Hernáiz's political activities during the months prior to the famous July 1830 Paris barricades revolt were confined to undercover work on behalf of Mina and Torrijos, though far away from the Spanish border as a result of a French order forbidding them from travelling south below Bordeaux, a city to which they journeyed briefly toward the end of 1829.

In the French summer elections of 1830, held on June 23 and July 3, Charles X and his supporters were routed. Then, in a badly miscalculated move to save the day, the King suspended freedom of the press and dissolved Parliament. The result was a popular upheaval, fueled by these measures of repression and further incited by the large newspapers *Le National, Le Temps* and *Le Globe* that refused to be silenced. Espronceda, forever the liberal crusader and rebel non pareil, is credited—though no mention of his name is made in the days' press accounts—by several of his biographers[2] with joining in the fray and fighting with unusual courage alongside Frenchmen against Charles' oppressive rule. If a change in the government with the ascension to power of Louis-Philippe meant a beneficial turn of climate for liberals in general and for Spanish emigrés in particular, Fernando VII saw the switch as dangerous to his own throne. Exiles could now operate freely from French territory and threaten his absolutist monarchy. From London such eminent leaders as Mendizábal, Alcalá Galiano and Palarea moved their residences to Paris. These and others, encouraged by the success of the July Revolution began seriously to plot the overthrow of the hated Fernando VII. Some travelled by sea to Gibraltar while others moved through southern France to try their fortune from the Pyrennees. Among the latter were Colonel Joaquín de Pablo and his men. A former leader of the Navarra volunteers, de Pablo was the first to cross the border into Spain in October of 1830 leading a group of two hundred men, among them Espronceda. On the 20th of October when they came up against General Eraso, commander of a two-thousand man force, de Pablo believed that his former compatriots would lay down their weapons and join him and his liberators. His words to them almost succeeded, but then a shot rang out and he fell dead from his mount. In spite of the valiant efforts by Espronceda and the rest of the men they were unable to rescue their leader's body from the royalist troops who proceeded to mutilate it, in the end impaling the head on a lance and exhibiting it in Pamplona's main square. Espronceda, who along with the leaderless group subsequently fled the numerically superior enemy, later commemorated this tragic episode of liberal resistance in the heroic poem, «A la muerte de Don Joaquín de Pablo (Chapalangarra).»

III. Love's Travails

Colonel Epifanio Mancha, his wife and their five children arrived in London on December 6, 1827, four months after Espronceda had done so. Thus it is plainly untrue that the poet recklessly followed his beloved as many would have it. Nevertheless, Espronceda could not have been unaware of her presence in London especially if his friendship with Don Epifanio in Lisbon had been as close as one is led to believe. Certainly the notice of February 1829 in *El Emigrado Observador*, London's Spanish newspaper, advertising: «Colonel Mancha's daughters will do beautiful embroidery, so as to derive from this activity the means by which to alleviate their financial indigency,» could not have escaped the young man. There can be little doubt but that the two lovers saw each other between the Mancha family's December arrival in London and Espronceda's departure for the Continent in February 1829, though no proof of such encounters exists. None of Espronceda's letters, to either his parents or his friends, mention Teresa by name or allude to any woman who could have been she. In 1829 Teresa was nineteen years old and, while fetchingly attractive, constituted a financial burden for her parents who struggled to feed, clothe and house a family of seven in a strange country, probably with only the help of the monthly pension allowed Spanish exiles. Inevitably the *bête noire* of every Romantic, a well-to-do bourgeois businessman, was given Teresa's hand in marriage. In March 1829, Gregorio del Bayo took Teresa for his wife in one of Summerstown's Catholic churches, probably Saint Eloise, thereby seemingly putting a stop to any further sentimental attachment between the two young lovers. A rich thirty-year-old Basque financier from Bilbao, del Bayo travelled widely and quite frequently throughout European capitals, most often to France. On one of these trips in May of 1830, whether accompanied by his new bride or not is uncertain, Gregorio stayed at the Favart Hotel where Espronceda also had his lodgings. The rivals, and possibly the lovers, met then for the first time after the marriage. The second time they met in the same hotel two years later, the outcome of the encounter was to be quite different from the formalities that characterized the first one.

Following the defeat of Joaquín de Pablo's handful of rebels in Navarra, Espronceda settled in Paris. Clearly regarded as a revolutionary by everyone who knew him, Espronceda remained in the French capital living on one-and-a-half francs a day from the government. At the beginning of the year 1831 he enlisted in a campaign organized in part by Victor Hugo to aid Poland in that country's struggle against Russia, and subsequently offered his services as a soldier, joining a force of French volunteers. The expedition, however, was forbidden to leave France by Louis Philippe who heeded the Czar's advice not to become involved in the conflict. Their attempt foiled and made to feel the French government's displeasure at their extended stay in the country, some Spaniards among those in the expeditionary division gathered at the Jean Jacques Rousseau Hotel to forge a tightly organized group which could effectively undermine Fernando's regime, now on a more amicable footing with Louis Philippe's. Espronceda had been selected as one of the speakers at his first public gathering, but preconceived plans came to very little since many of the more respected exiles, Angel Saavedra (the future Duke of Rivas), the Count of Toreno, and Alcalá Galiano, among them, boycotted a movement they considered ineffectual. Leaflets were distributed and the scheming continued on the part of the diehards until the French government, tired of the unrest their gatherings were provoking and no doubt urged by Fernando VII to curb their activities, began to place mounting objections to their assemblies and fund raisings. Finally, when in September 1830 these tireless Spanish patriots filed into government offices to pick up their monthly support money, they were obliged to pledge a discontinuance of their insurrectionist plots against Fernando VII and to leave Paris prior to the middle of the month. Those who refused to sign the document placed before them lost not only their sole means of support but all of their civil liberties as well. Espronceda was one of those who found himself sent to Bordeaux. Before leaving in November for this southern city, he visited the Countess of Torrijos in whose husband's service he had been engaged several times. Not finding the lady at home he left a poem for her, a tender epistolar ballad, «Yo sé que estás enojada . . . ,» apologizing for an unkept promise, the nature of which remains puzzling to this day.

In Bordeaux Espronceda remained a little over two months. Once again he showed up in England in February 1832. Disenchanted with the ill fortunes befallen him in the realm of politics, Espronceda turned his attention once more to love and personal intrigue. Infatuated still with the memory of Teresa, by now married and truly a forbidden fruit, he sought her out persistently until the two became lovers again, agreeing one night at a party to flee London and leave behind forever the hapless Gregorio del Bayo. Unable to find the propitious moment, their elopement was postponed several times. Finally, in October 1832 Espronceda knowingly awaited in Paris at the Favart Hotel the arrival of the del Bayos. On the night of October 16, Teresa, forsaking her husband and their two children, stole away silently with her lover to a second-floor apartment on Panorama Street. A few weeks later they moved to a small house on the outskirts.

Not only had love begun to smile on Espronceda, but in Madrid on October 15, 1832, the Regent for an ailing Fernando VII, his fourth wife María Cristina, issued a proclamation of amnesty for those exiles and political prisoners formerly persecuted by the King. Politically, then, Espronceda had plenty of reason to be happy and so, jointly with Teresa, began to plan their return to Spain. Espronceda crossed the border into Spanish soil by himself around the first of March 1833, and Teresa followed some three weeks later.

IV. The Return to Life in Spain

In his family's Madrid home José found only his mother. Don Juan had died earlier that year on January 1 at the age of eighty-three. Espronceda settled down to live alone with his mother and proceeded to reacquaint himself with old friends, especially those at «El Parnasillo,» the literary society which met at a cafe next to the Príncipe Theater. Mesonero Romanos, the greatest *costumbrista* writer of his time describes the gatherings of these young Romantics in their evening sessions, animated by verse readings and far-fetched ideas coming from the likes of Larra, Bretón de los Herreros, Gil y Zárate, Ventura de la Vega, Zorrilla, Campoamor, García Gutiérrez, Hartzenbusch, Estébanez Calderón and, of course, Espronceda at the dimly lit and poorly furnished locale inappropriately called «Café del Príncipe.»[3]

Largely unoccupied, Espronceda began considering at this juncture a possible military career for himself. An opportunity to enter the armed forces and follow in his father's footsteps presented itself when, in May 1833, he was offered a post as a member of the Royal Guard Corps. His tenure in the elite troops did not last long since, imprudently enough, he was accused of composing and then reading one night at a banquet a poem containing pointedly derrogatory remarks about the King who, though terminally ill, retained a certain amout of power. Expelled from the Royal Guards for his subversive poetry, Espronceda was once again banished from Madrid because of his liberalism and his record as a former emigré instigator. This time he was shipped off to the city of Cuéllar. Happily, also once again, his watchdog in exile was not too convinced of the gravity of the offense committed. He turned out to be none other than one of the co-founders of the old «Los Numantinos» group, Miguel Ortiz, now lord mayor of this small town in Old Castile.

The summer of 1833 was thus spent away from his mother's house in

Madrid and from Teresa who lived in an apartment in the next building. Having failed to secure an income of his own, Espronceda then twenty-five, began to write with an eye to earning money, even though his mother seems to have had enough of an income from real estate properties for them to live very comfortably. The book on which he worked in this quiet Segovian town was the novel *Sancho Saldaña o El Castellano de Cuéllar*, a historical yarn running to six volumes and which he indeed succeeded in selling to the publisher Manuel Delgado for a considerable amount of money upon his return to Madrid in the winter of 1832-33.

V. Literature and Politics

When Fernando VII died on September 24, 1833, leaving behind a torn nation and the building of the Prado Museum as his sole memorable accomplishment, Espronceda resumed his life in Madrid. Writing, political intrigue and love placed equal demands upon his time. With Bernardino Núñez de Arenas, Ros de Olano, Ventura de la Vega and García de Villalta he made his debut in the literary scene with the publication of the journal *El Siglo*, a bi-weekly (Tuesdays and Fridays) that broke with tradition from the time its first number appeared on the stands on January 21, 1834, when Martínez de la Rosa was inaugurated as Prime Minister. In the magazine, frequently sequestered by the censorship authorities, Espronceda and his colleagues published their ultra-liberal editorials as well as poems which had nothing to do with political circumstance such as the former's «Himno al sol,» «Fresca, lozana, pura y olorosa» and «Despedida del patriota griego de la hija del apóstata.» Espronceda published other poems here, anonymously at times, though when these took any sort of a blatant political stance they were usually blanked out entirely by the censors, save for the title, as it happened with his already mentioned «A la muerte de Don Joaquín de Pablo (Chapalangarra).» In fact the journal's last issue, published March 7, 1834, appeared totally blank except for headlines and titles. This effective maneuver aroused the anger of the police who searched in vain for those responsible, but it signified also, by official decree, the end of *El Siglo*.

On May 11, 1834, a daughter was born to Teresa and Espronceda. She was given the name of Blanca like the name of the heroine of her father's tragedy *Blanca de Borbón* already written by that time but which remained unpublished until 1870, long after his death, and has never been staged. Another play, done in collaboration with his friend Antonio Ros de Olano,

Ni el tío ni el sobrino had premiered earlier that year on April 25. A comedy of manners, it lasted on the stage only three days before it was taken off amid public apathy and lukewarn reviews even by such friends of the dramatist as Larra. Espronceda's conspiratorial activities, especially his part in *El Siglo's* harassment of Martínez de la Rosa's government and his membership in «La Isabelina,» a secret society that urged the adoption of the old liberal Constitution of 1812 of Cádiz and which had been founded by the Aviraneta immortalized by Baroja, landed the poet in jail in the early morning hours of July 25, 1834. Though released soon afterward as a result of a letter he wrote to the Queen—published by *Revista Española* on August 12—pleading for his freedom, Espronceda was a *persona non grata* to a conservative, if tottering, government and consequently his third forced exile began, probably in August of that same year, in Badajoz. By September, however, Espronceda was nowhere near his place of banishment, instead he had travelled south to Andalucía where he ran out of funds and had to write to his friend Balbino Cortés for a loan. The government's intent had been to merely remove the troublemaker from Madrid for a while, so no punitive action against him was instituted. Chances are, then, that by the time the last volume of his novel *Sancho Saldaña* went on sale in November, Espronceda was back in Madrid attesting to Martínez de la Rosa's untenability as head of the government.

With the advent of 1835 there came to Spain a chaotic situation of ever-worsening proportions: the festering civil war started by the Carlists who supported the brother of Fernando VII, Don Carlos and his claim to the throne, against the deceased King's daughter, Isabel. Economically, socially and politically the country marched on a disastrous course which not even a new government headed by the Count of Toreno could do much to reverse. Madrid continued in a civil turmoil aggravated by a cholera epidemic, and in August, with Espronceda assuming a leading role, another uprising began to do away with Toreno's government which collapsed almost immediately. One of his more progressive ministers, Juan Alvarez Mendizábal, then took over the reins aided by the support of the many liberal groups milling around Madrid in the mid 1830s. Espronceda and others of his convictions benefited from Mendizábal's policies, sometimes directly and in an official way, as for example the poet's mission to Andalucía in the capacity of political envoy of the government. This is a far cry from Espronceda's earlier political activities of conspiracy and open revolt, marking the beginning—within his lifelong involvement in the political continuum—of Espronceda's movements within a lawful perimeter. It turned out to be a tentative departure from his old self. Another step back into rebellious opposition was yet to come before

Espronceda would remain in the mainstreams of active government service. Mendizábal's promises of reform, once he found himself in power, could not be implemented as fully as he had anticipated and therefore his most vocal supporters began to desert him. Even Espronceda broke openly with the government he had backed with such enthusiasm when he wrote the essay *El Ministerio Mendizábal*. This impassioned piece symbolized the growing power of the press, whose influence on public opinion ultimately led to the resignation of a Prime Minister who had governed Spain for a mere eight months, from September 14, 1835, to May 15, 1836.

VI. Love and Loss

No one had denied the impetuosity with which Espronceda loved Teresa, but equally true was his inconstancy toward her. Having abandoned her husband and two young children for him, Teresa must have felt more than slighted while living alone in an apartment next to her lover's house, at being paraded through Madrid streets as though she were a prize that had been won, and at having to endure his prolonged and frequent absences. Teresa wanted a life and a home with the man who had enamoured her so completely that she had destroyed her past for a chance of a future with him; albeit Espronceda was content with their segregated life style. Her beauty, which attracted many among Espronceda's friends, provided Teresa with the means to anesthetize the anger and the jealousy she increasingly felt. Unable to curb his passions for politics, literature and other diversions, Teresa threw herself at one of her admirers, promising to run away with him if he would only kill the ingrate. Finding her offer spurned, Teresa fled by herself to Valladolid where she remained until Espronceda arrived to take her back to Madrid. The relationship, though momentarily rekindled, did not last following this deliberate break. Espronceda, immersed in politics—at times paying for his excesses in jail, at others busy organizing demonstrations, giving speeches or writing incendiary editorials—could not cope with Teresa's demands. Politically she was becoming a liability; emotionally, he had changed. Their love, he no doubt came to feel, had been a flash—intense but ephemeral and unsustainable.

Their last quarrel took place in a police detective's house on Flora Street where Espronceda had hidden previously during the revolts against Istúriz, and where also he had written «El Verdugo» and «El Mendigo.» Here Teresa walked out a bitter and destitute woman, leaving the poet with their daughter Blanca whom his mother Doña Carmen looked after with all the affection expected of a grandmother until the girl's marriage to Narciso de la Escosura, a friend of her father. Teresa's life, in ruins since their escape to Spain, was further shattered following this last confrontation. For a while she lived with former friends of Espronceda and then, tired and ill, fell into a life of prostitution until she died tuberculose at the age of twenty-nine.

On the night of September 18, 1839, as Espronceda strolled home alone from an evening out, he was struck by the sight of an open window in this chilly autumn darkness on the ground floor of number 22 Santa Isabel Street. Surrounded by candles there lay in state the body of his estranged Teresa whom he had loved so deeply in past years. The shock of the moment and definitive loss of someone so close are reflected in the second Canto of his unfinished *El Diablo Mundo*. The elegy he titled «Canto a Teresa,» however, turns out to be an execration of the lost woman as a whore-madonna culpable of all of his misfortunes in love.[4]

Espronceda's health, never very good—unlike his father's long and vigorous life—worsened during this time, aggravated by the turn of events in the last year with Teresa. Consequently, from at least 1838 on, his participation in politics, though as intensely genuine as before, became more judicious and restrained. Periodically ill, during a period of convalescence he was visited by the young José Zorrilla, the future author of the super-romantic *Don Juan Tenorio*. Zorrilla in his memoirs, *Recuerdos del tiempo viejo*, portrayed Espronceda shortly after Teresa gave him up (February 1834) thusly:

> La cabeza de Espronceda rebosaba carácter y originalidad. Su cara, pálida, por la enfermedad, estaba coronada por una cabellera negra, riza y sedosa, dividida por una raya casi en medio de la cabeza, y ahuecada por ambos lados sobre las orejas, pequeñas y finas, cuyos lóbulos inferiores asomaban entre rizos. Sus cejas negras, finas y rectas, doselaban sus ojos límpidos e inquietos, resguardados por riquísimas pestañas; el perfil de su nariz no era muy correcto; y su boca, desdeñosa, cuyo labio inferior era algo aborbonado, estaba medio oculta en un fino bigote y una perilla unida a la barba, que se rizaba por ambos lados de la mandíbula inferior. Su frente era espaciosa y sin más rayas que las que, de arriba abajo, marcaba el fruncimiento de las cejas; su mirada era franca, y su risa, pronta y frecuente, no rompía jamás en descompuesta carcajada. Su cuello era vigoroso y sus manos finas, nerviosas y bien cuidadas.[5]

This impressionistic portrait of Espronceda, then twenty-nine years old faithfully corresponds to the better-known paintings and lithographs depicting the poet at the height of his fame and characterizes the essential Espronceda recognizable by everyone.

In 1838, together with Eugenio Moreno López, Espronceda tried his hand again at playwriting. The result was the drama *Amor venga sus agravios* publicized under the pseudonym Luis Senra y Palomares, staged for the first time on September 28, and received as cooly as his earlier *Ni el tío ni el sobrino*. Together with *Blanca de Borbón* this was his last attempt at producing anything for the theater.

In spite of the repeated failures as a dramatist, Espronceda's fame continued climbing in every quarter. By this time he had published his most celebrated poem, «La canción del pirata,» as well as others equally memorable: «El reo de muerte,» «El canto del cruzado,» and the long dramatic verse composition *El Estudiante de Salamanca*. His position at the forefront of the men of letters of his day brought him an invitation to join the board of directors of the Liceo Artístico y Literario, a Madrid cultural society that rivaled the Ateneo in prestige and in whose magazine of the same name Espronceda published several of his best known verses. The next year he was given the post of lecturer of the society's modern comparative literature seminar. His friend Enrique Gil y Carrasco, whom we know today as a novelist and poet but who was better regarded as a perceptive critic in his day, reviewed Espronceda's first lecture on poetics. Gil's impression was that though his ideas offered merited consideration, their dishevelled organization and random structuring detracted from Espronceda's total presentation.[6] Clearly recorded, however, stands his position that poetry, far from being a means through which one merely excites the senses, should be thought of as a vehicle for noble ideas capable of filling men's hearts,[7] a credo Espronceda remained faithful to throughout his life. His verse, though not always a container of noble ideals, scarcely a model of Art for Art's sake, has much in common with *engagé* poetry.

VII. Legitimacy, Respectability and Fame

In the realm of politics, the years 1838-39 mark Espronceda's plunge into the pursuit of elective office. According to the July 23, 1838, issue of the daily *El Mundo* he finished rather poorly in the race for the House of Representatives seat from Badajoz. This minor setback did not seem to deter Espronceda from his aspirations. That same year he toured Granada, Málaga and Cádiz on a campaign that included his conferring with powerful political *caciques,* seeking their support. The banquet circuit provided a podium for his political views which, still as liberal as ever, were softened by his popular appeal as the most-touted poet of the times and one of the most admired young politicos of Madrid. Declaring himself a republican, the faction that opposed the Regent Queen, Espronceda joined forces with the revolutionary newspaper *El Huracán,* notorious for its intractable editorials and denigrations of establishment politicians. If the alliance provided Espronceda with another forum, it also proved beneficial to the paper which the poet defended in a court of law against charges derived from its subversive harangues. His arguments proved convincing enough to win a dismissal of the accusations levelled by the government prosecutor. The death of his mother on October 29, 1840, one and one-half weeks later, prevented Espronceda from savoring this latest triumph for very long. Her passing away also signaled a large change in his lifestyle. He no longer felt able to properly look after his daughter, Blanca, and sent her as a boarder to the finest girl's school in Madrid located on Hortaleza Street.

By now Espronceda had become an important personnage in the nation's capital. He was widely recognized as—in today's vernacular—a «personality.» Whether he took himself seriously as such or not, he clearly enjoyed the image and did not shy away from affairs, intrigues of various sorts or even duels, all of which enhanced his aura of a talented *bon vivant.* In one of his less fortunate encounters, where he was not even supposed to be a participant, he suffered a broken clavicle. Originally, the poet and his good friend, Juan de la Pezuela, Count of Cheste, were to serve as witnesses to a duel fought with swords between Andrés Borrego and Luis González Bravo over a political disagreement. Somehow in the course of the fight Espronceda's friendship with Pezuela turned into enmity through partisan encouragement of the duelists. The two parted enemies, having previously agreed to meet behind the San Martín graveyard to settle matters with swords. The sole witness to the episode was Espronceda's companion General Ros de Olano who did not want to see the poet hurt and neither did his opponent, a full colonel in the cavalry and a practiced swordsman. Yet after wounding Espronceda in his right hand in an attempt to avert further bloodshed and end the duel honorably, Pezuela was forced, seeing his own life imperilled by the other's aggresiveness, to stop him with a thrust to the upper chest.

VIII. Death and Posthumous Fame

Conspirator, traveller, revolutionary, abductor, duelist, all these personae behind him, Espronceda reached the year 1840 hoping to channel his life into the two parallel courses of literature and politics, but within a more traditional, organized and accepted context. The end of the first Carlist War resulted in the abdication of the Regent María Cristina, who went into exile in Marseilles, and the ascension to power of Baldomero Espartero, one of the conquering heroes of the conflict. During General Espartero's tenure in office, a relatively short one (May 10, 1841 to July 23, 1843), Espronceda lived his final period of political involvement. Thankfully, Espartero, a progressive ruler who styled himself a liberal, recognizing Espronceda's deeply held commitment to liberal ideals and the esteem in which the public held him, named the poet Secretary to Spain's embassy in the Low Countries in November 1841. Whether in fact Espartero was repaying Espronceda for the June 8, 1840 congratulatory manifesto in praise of his victories which the poet signed with others and may have authored,[8] or whether he was simply trying to rid himself of an extremist among his own staff of supporters by assigning Espronceda to a prestigious but far away post, one can only conjecture. Espartero had ample cause for both, and here he found an opportunity to achieve the latter while appearing to do the former. The trouble is that the ploy, if indeed it was one, worked only a matter of days[9] because Espronceda finally found himself elected as Representative from the province of Almería and wasted no time in returning from The Hague. On March 1, 1842, Espronceda took his seat for the first time in the Spanish *Cortes.* He attended to his parliamentary duties with admirable assiduousness and the chamber's record shows his active participation in diverse issues: taxes and import quotas, laws governing the press and the church, military mobilization and the draft. The Madrid dailies commenting on the performance of the freshman legistator remark on an understandable initial lack of self-confidence in such august surroundings, but point out as well his grasp of the issues, his measured responses and his constructive remarks on the matters under discussion.

Espronceda's last days in public were between May 15, when he attended an evening gala given by the Regent Espartro, and the 17th, as he occupied his place in Parliament. He fell ill the next day after travelling on horseback to Aranjuez, a summer residence community for the well-to-do located a few miles south of Madrid, where he had gone to visit his bride to be, Bernarda de Beruete. After five days Espronceda died from what was then diagnosed as a respiratory ailment, perhaps the croup, but which today is widely believed to have been diphtheria. He was buried the next day, May 24, 1842, at the San Nicolás cementery in mid-afternoon, accompanied by a brillant and numerous retinue of Madrid literati and government and religious leaders, headed by his uncle the Bishop of Córdoba and the Count of Las Navas. His remains were then transferred sixty years later to the Panteón de Hombres Ilustres del Siglo XIX.

Espronceda's literary and personal fame, clearly undiminished since his death, began its rise in 1840 with the publication of the installments of *El Diablo Mundo* and the collection of his poems, already well known by then, in the volume *Poesías* dedicated to Carmen Osorio. With this woman, a beautiful married Madrid socialite, Espronceda had an affair for some time following the wane of Teresa's muse. The lady's fickle reputation together with the discretion of Espronceda's friends, among them his first biographers, have obscured further details of the relationship, though its importance cannot de denied in view of the volume's veiled dedication to Mrs. Osorio in the initial poem, the sonnet «A xxx dedicándole estas poesías.»

His political maturation and the consolidation of his reputation as a poet of the first order not unexpectedly mirror the tenor of Espronceda's third and last great love. Unlike Teresa or Carmen, Bernarda de Beruete was neither a passionate lover nor a courtly seductress. A woman of considerable wealth, she did not allow herself to be carried away easily by Espronceda's undeniable charm or his notable prestige. In the end, however, she fell under his influence and accepted his proposal of marriage. The courtship evolved slowly in the tranquil and socially conventional manner which Bernarda observed. As its incipient moments, the impatience aroused in Espronceda by her touching reticence is revealed in this love note:

> Ver a usted y no amarla es casi imposible; pero sí lo es del todo el poder hablarla, si usted no facilita la ocasión. Estoy seguro de que usted no accederá a la súplica que le hago de que me proporcione una; pero no dude usted de que, en mi situación, prefiero una realidad funesta a la terrible incertidumbre en que vivo. A usted toca desvanecerla. Sea cual fuere la resolución de usted, podrá extinguirse la esperanza, pero nunca el aprecio y cariño que inspira a su apasionado.[10]

As Bernarda wished, and allowed, their love grew toward the date of their wedding, set unfortunately for several months after the poet's premature death. Though completely shunted from her lover's side during his final days, due to the straight-laced morality of the times, Bernarda mourned him for the rest of her life. Dressed in black, she walked often to his grave at San Nicolás where a fresh bouquet of flowers was placed devotedly for years.

That Esproncedo's life constituted the stuff from which legends are made there can be no doubt. Mourned by sycophants who enshrined him in early hagiographies, studied and analyzed by critics of his life and works for a century and-a-half, Espronceda also became the protagonist of more fictional literature than any other poet in the history of Spanish letters.[11] Pérez Galdós had him appear in several of his *Episodios Nacionales: Los apostólicos, Mendizábal, De Oñate a La Granja, La estafeta romántica*, and *Bodas reales*. Patricio de la Escosura's Eduardo de la Flor, hero of his novel *El patriarca del valle*, is none other than his close personal friend Espronceda. In the twentieth century, Pío Baroja cast him in no less than eight of the volumes of his *Memorias de un hombre de acción*, especially *La veleta de Garastizar, Los caudillos de 1830,* and *la Isabelina*; Valle Inclán refers to him in the *Sonata de Otoño*. Finally, Rosa Chacel makes no attempt to disguise Espronceda's most tempestuous love affair in her novel *Teresa* published in 1941.

Legendary even in his own time, today Espronceda remains the most memorable of the unforgettable generation of Spanish Romantics. Alive not only through his own work but in that of others, Espronceda challenges us as a fictional and as a historical figure; simultaneously author and character.

NOTES

1. Robert Marrast, *José de Espronceda et son temps* (Paris, 1974), p. 140.

2. *Ibid.,* p. 155.

3. Cited by Esteban Pujals, *Espronceda y Lord Byron* (Madrid, 1972), pp. 70-71. See also Jean-Louis Picoche, *Un romántico español: Enrique Gil y Carrasco* (Madrid, 1978), pp. 32-33.

4. Ricardo López Landeira, «La desilusión poética de Espronceda: Realidad y poesía irreconciliables,» *Boletín de la Real Academia Española* 55 (Mayo-agosto 1975), 324-28, and Bruce W. Wardropper, «Espronceda's *Canto a Teresa* and the Spanish Elegiac Tradition,» *Bulletin of Hispanic Studies*, 4 (1963), 89-100.

5. Cited by Esteban Pujals, *op. cit.,* pp. 73-74.

6. Cited in José Espronceda, *Poesías líricas y fragmentos épicos,* Robert Marrast, ed. (Madrid, 1970), p. 20. All subsequent page and verse references correspond to this edition.

7. *Ibid.,* p. 20.

8. *Ibid.,* p. 21.

9. In his edition of José de Espronceda, *El Estudiante de Salamanca* (Boston,

1919), George T. Northrup writes that «In November, 1841, he /Esproncedaʃ accepted an appointment to serve as secretary to the Spanish legation at The Hague. He served in this capacity exactly five days. Arriving at The Hague on January 29, 1842, he departed for Madrid on February 3, 1842» (p. xviii).

10.   Pujals, *op. cit.,* p. 81.

11.   José de Espronceda, *Obras completas de D. José de Espronceda*, Jorge Campos, ed. (Madrid, 1954), p. xi.

CHAPTER TWO

Romanticism and Spain

Romanticism, perhaps the last of the great cultural movements that affected the entire western world, manifested itself in almost every facet of public endeavor: architecture and literature, politics and fashions, sculpture and painting, philosophy and theology. The phenomenon began in England and Germany in the 1790s, spreading two decades later to France and subsequently to other European countries, Italy, Spain, and Poland, which can be said to have had no indigenous romantic movements but rather to have imported a derivative version of the German and English romantic revolts.

I. Static Mechanism versus Dynamic Organicism

In the late eighteenth century part of the world came to an end. An intellectual dissatisfaction toppled the static metaphysical structure which man had accepted since Plato. Labelled «static mechanism» by Prof. Morse Peckham in a brilliant essay[1] based on Arthur O. Lovejoy's *The Great Chain of Being* (Harvard, 1936), it describes how man had for centuries conceived the universe to be a perfect and orderly machine, hierarchical, inmutable and completed, with no inconsistencies or imperfections except for those things beyond his ability to fully comprehend. And, as Peckham wrote in March 1951, «For most people it still remains the unrealized base for most of their values, intellectual, moral, social, aesthetic, and religious.»[2] The glaring lacunae of inconsistencies of such a deist system, however, flawed it so irrevocably for those no longer content with a rationally untenable position that, left unattended and defenseless, it simply crumbled. In its place a new order came into being, a metaphysics founded on the concept of an organism, something alive and forever growing, not a machine. Change therefore became a virtue and growth an expected and ongoing process. Whereas perfection had been considered an inherent quality of the mechanistic system, as a finished and closed philosophy, flaws became a virtue due to the unattainability of perfection save for ephemeral moments that succeed each other in a great chain of relationships and changes. «Dynamic organicism,» as Peckham called it, turned the universe into something alive, growing, changing and, logically, imperfect.

The cataclysmic change met with the expected resistance from the traditional bastions of the status quo: the Church for whom the new system implied a god who, along with the rest of the universe, had a beginning and at best was becoming less imperfect every day; and the national governments, threatened by the dislocation of all the social and moral conventions that constitute the basis for stability and continuity. In spite of its apocalyptic significance, dynamic organicism initially touched a small few—but radically so, and ultimately these men who understood it spread the new order among the rest. In the beginning, finding themselves disinfranchised from a comfortable theodicy, the eighteenth-century intellectuals sought a way out of their self-inflicted chaos and doubt. This initial period of disorientation called, again by Peckham, «negative romanticism,» is characterized by a despair of finding an ultimate meaning in life, by a feeling of cosmic isolation and a guilt from which not even reason can extricate the individual. Some, such as Lord Byron, managed to create under this kind of a burden, though their works reflect the anguish they toiled under. Most Romantics, however, went through the initial stage as though it were a development period in which little of the desolation, never totally forgotten, was overcome. Adaptable beings that men are, the Romantics eventually reconciled themselves to the metaphysics of organic dynamicism, thereby feeling a part of the universal order. In other words, they made peace with the universe, but not with society. Their alienation from it, irreconcialably deep, embittered many if not most of them, turning some into rebels and others into outcasts. This is the productive period known as «positive romanticism»[3] when the great majority of the Romantics wrote their poetry, their dramas and their novels. Most, finally able to function artistically, combine elements from both periods. Romantic literature reflects such attitudes in its glorifications of corsairs, bastards, executioners, beggars and other considered undesirables by society, and by its exaggerated sentimentality, a belief in the power of fate, the exoticism of distant lands of time past, and foremost by the assertion of the individual who more often than not is the poet himself.

II. The Nature of Spanish Romanticism

When Romanticism came to Spain, almost half a century had passed since its first stirrings in the Germany and England of the 1790s. Few in Spain had paid any attention to the cultural movement, and specifically its literary manifestations, then sweeping Europe, until the year 1814[4] when the German Consul in Cádiz Johan Nikolas Böhl von Faber published the article «Reflexiones de Schlegel sobre el teatro traducidas del alemán.» It appeared on September 14, 1814, in the local paper *Mercurio Gaditano*, and it was, aside from a rendering of Schlegel's views of Spanish and English drama, essentially a defense of traditional Spanish ballads and the theater of Calderón, both considered «romantic» by the Germans. The piece prompted a quick reply from the critic and poet José Joaquín de Mora who disputed the merits of Romanticism, quarrelled with the identification of Calderón and the *Romancero* with the rest of Spanish literature, and in the meanwhile, extolled Neoclassicism in a frazzled rhetoric. The polemic, joined in by the likes of Antonio Alcalá Galiano, who began by supporting Mora but later defended Romanticism, went on for nearly four years. Historically it can be said to have had a place in the advent of Romanticism into Spain if only because it divulged the concept across the pages of many newspapers in Cádiz and Madrid. Ultimately, however, it was an inconsequential debate because neither the proponents nor the detractors of the new wave knew very much about it and contributed little if anything to its development. And nobody won in the controversy because the coming of Romanticism into Spain at that juncture was inevitable, unless of course, as Edmund L. King put it, «Böhl's election to the /Spanish Royal/ Academy /in 1820/ can be considered the prize.»[5]

Spanish Romanticism is different from European Romanticism in its manifestations, nature and proliferacy, and more importantly because Spanish Romantics, even though they may have behaved no differently than their European counterparts, did not possess a full conscious awareness of their romantic bent. Theirs was little more than an attitude,[6] thus they could neither explain nor resolve what I believe is the crux of all Romantics: the dislocation extant between reality as they perceived it and as they wished it to be. In Espronceda we can distinguish a trajectory suggesting an increasing realization of the abyss separating what he as a poet could fantasize and what he as a man had within his reach. He was confronted with a fundamental incongruence between vital posture and artistic manifestation. The awareness of this imbalance—the imaginable versus the attainable—led Espronceda to despair; first, because he felt incapable of bridging the distance that separates them and, second, because he could not adjust his desires to the possibilities before him. Herein lies the inherent contradiction of Romanticism, of an art incongruent with the poet's experience.

While Romanticism does not imply the same thing in all countries, even among European ones,[7] by and large the Spanish brand shares with all others the traits that follow. Grouped together they offer an approximate, not a definitive, formulation of what I interpret as Spanish Romanticism.

1. The essential characteristic of Romanticism is its blatant egocentrism. The poet's ego and exalted personality dominate all other considerations. Nature becomes a mere projection of his personal sentiments, at the very least their extension, giving rise to a plethora of pathetic fallacies where land- and sea-scapes reflect subjectively the poet's inner self. The thunder and lightning that score the protagonist's plunge to death into a remote chasm, amid his proferred blasphemies in Rivas' *Don Alvaro o la fuerza del sino,* provides a good example.

2. Whereas the Neoclassics hid their sentiments in favor of their ideas, the Romantics instituted an aesthetics of sensual, impassioned, violent and terrifying emotions. Melancholy, despair and solitary sadness are the attributes we can ascribe to the Romantics. The whistling of a forest wind, a ciaroscuro graveyard illuminated by the moon, the pounding of the surf upon a deserted beach, an abandoned castle in ruins, all these stereotyped romantic scenarios reflect the somber disposition of the hero.

3. Freedom of every sort became the rallying cry of all Romantics. Passion displaced reason whether in politics or in art. Absolutist rulers such as Charles X of France and Fernando VII of Spain were replaced by governments in which a segment of the citizenry at least appeared to have some say. In the realm of literature and other creative arts the old canons fell by the wayside. The poet, with a narcissistic reliance on his imagination and emotions, beheld no other model than himself. In poetry, new rhyme schemes and polymetry as well as a renewed interest in venerable meters such as the ballad dominate. In drama the three unities of time, space and action are discarded, and a deliberate confusion of tragedy and comedy together with prose and verse appear in the best known plays.

4. As a result of the radical metaphysical shift to dynamic organicism which affected most Romantics to some degree, the vacuum left by the

overthrow of the comfortable static mechanism of old was felt very keenly. The notion of a limitless universe, forever growing, meant an unknowable fate for them as mortal beings, shattering the romantics and making them look upon life as an unending enigma, disquieting and hostile. Their touchstone was their idealism but even here they could find no firm foothold: the ideal woman turned out to have feet of clay, their country exiled them, their fellowmen ostracized them. Finding everything beyond reality's reach, some rebelled like Espronceda, some committed suicide like Larra and some emigrated like the Duke of Rivas. Escapism of a lesser sort, whether into the underworld of drugs, far away places such as the Orient, or ancient times such as the medieval settings of their writings attracted the Romantics.

5.   The leitmotifs of romantic literature faithfully reflect the poet's temper: a) landscape, no longer the bucolic *locus amoenus* («nice place») where shepherds sat while composing idyllic love laments, shows interest as a living thing, antagonistic at times, at others pantheistically meaningful such as in Bécquer's short story «Los ojos verdes,» always alive like any other character; b) the revelations of the poet's innermost feelings, as he sheds layer after layer in Romanticism's genre par excellence, the lyric poem; c) the affirmation of national and regional values, such as the subliterature of *costumbrismo,* gain favor as a result of political and indivudial preferences; d) the legends derived from distant lands and long-ago periods (e.g. the Crusades, medieval knights and troubadors) serve to inspire countless pages; e) political and ideological considerations engender many circumstantial compositions but also result in some of the best romantic poetry as seen in Espronceda's own «Canción del pirata,» «A Chapalangarra,» or «El 2 de mayo»; f) destiny or blind fate, oblivious to man's lot on earth, appears as the force against which we are all powerless.

6.   Romantic style, strident and often convulsed, was conditioned by two factors: the poet's own dynamic personality and the public for which it was intended, the masses. In detriment to harmony and measure, exaggerated sentimentality and sonorous rhymes took over. Goya's *Caprichos* or Espronceda's «A Jarifa en una orgía» employ this type of violent style meant to shock and provoke a public largely apathetic upon whom, gone the era of maecenas, romantic artists depended for a living.

III. The Unfolding of Spanish Romanticism

The critic Agustín Durán published in 1828 his *Discurso sobre el influ-*

jo que ha tenido la crítica moderna en la decadencia del teatro antiguo español. This treatise defends, once again, the Golden Age theater of Lope de Vega and Calderón as uniquely Spanish in its exalted nationalism, thus tacitly endorsing Böhl von Faber's defense of the Shlegel brothers' romantic interpretation of traditional Spanish literature. Other proponents of Romanticism followed after 1828 such as Juan Donoso Cortés who, deviating some from the first two scholars, spoke of a European Romanticism, more liberal, Christian and historical than the uniquely Spanish one. In the prologue to his 1830 novel *Los bandos de Castilla*, Ramón López Soler defended the romantic historical novel as conceived by Walter Scott (whose *Ivanhoe* he plagiarized here) and Romanticism because they fulfilled the ideals of solitude, sensibility and alienation. Lastly Alcalá Galiano, in the unsigned introduction to his friend the Duke of Rivas' *El moro expósito*, wrote in 1834 a highly critical essay against the already floundering Spanish and French neo-classical period, calling it unoriginal, cold and superficial. These critics and others whose words no longer matter are the sole theoreticians of Spanish Romanticism at the time of its early dawnings. Though their writings did not reach definitive critically formulated proportions, they, nevertheless, served to introduce and nurture a new literary sensibility in the 1830s and early 1840s in Spain.

Within the general romantic movement two distinct phases have been noted, a «negative» and a «positive» Romanticism as Peckham wished to call them. Somewhat attentuated in Spain, these two modes, rather than constituting developmental stages where the first one leads into the second, coexisted almost from the very beginning. Negative Spanish Romanticism, characterized by a revolutionary liberalism, sought to erect from ground zero a new social as well as an original cultural order. Its leaders were Larra and Espronceda. On the other hand, positive Spanish Romanticism sought, by looking back on Spain's chivalrous Middle Ages, its Christian Gothic, and its Golden Age literature, to glorify traditional values, not to destroy or ignore them. Enrique Gil y Carrasco and José Zorrilla were its proponents. Rivas belongs more to this second group given his preference for historical themes and his conformity with traditional literary conventions, though the counter-Christian and frenzied emotionalist ethos that pervade *Don Alvaro* do give some pause.

While Alcalá Galiano looked upon Germany as Romanticism's birth place, Spains's version was imported primarily from France, in spite of the unquestionable fact that Walter Scott's translators and imitators for a time fared better in Spain than either native original Spanish writings or French translations of Hugo and Chateaubriand put together. In France Romanticism had reached its zenith with the 1830 Revolution and the premiere of

Hugo's *Hernani*. The latter's *Préface du 'Cromwell'*, French literature's romantic manifesto, probably inspired Alcalá Galiano's own preface to Rivas' *El moro expósito* which, significantly, was published in Paris. This long (14,000 hendecasyllabic verses) poem, based on the medieval Castilian legend of the seven scions of Lara, a bloody tale of revenge and intrigue,* marks the true inauguration of Spanish Romanticism even though it first appeared in France. Other critics, mindful of the poem's foreign first edition, bestow the honor on another work by the same author, a drama staged on Sunday, May 22 of the following year in Madrid's Teatro del Príncipe titled *Don Alvaro o la fuerza del sino*. The work, Rivas' and perhaps Spanish Romanticism's most important play, represents an emotional tour de force where Don Alvaro and Leonor, the lover protagonists, separated time and again by seemingly adverse fate, meet horrible deaths—she, at the hands of her brother don Alfonso, and he, taking his own life while asking Hell's welcome. The play, a box office success, was without a doubt Romanticism's resounding public debut in Spain.

The first phase of Spanish Romanticism ended with the momentous success of *Don Alvaro*. It had been up to that time a trasitorial period where José Cadalso with his *Noches lúgubres,* Meléndez Valdés and his sentimental nature poetry, Jovellanos and the liberal idealism of his patriotic essays, Martínez de la Rosa with his melancholy erotic *Poesías*, and the corrosive essays of Larra prepared the way for a decade and a half of prodigious output of genuinely romantic theater, poetry and, to a much lesser extent, novel.

To the second stage belong the trimuph of *Don Alvaro* and the vibrant poetry of Espronceda, collected five years after the staging of Rivas' masterpiece in a thin volume entitled simply *Poesías*. From 1834 until the early 1840s we find a veritable treasury of romantic jewels: Espronceda's *Sancho Saldaña o El Castellano de Cuéllar* was published in 1834; Martínez de la Rosa's *La conjuración de Venecia* was algo staged in the same year; likewise Larra's *El doncel de don Enrique el Doliente* and his *Artículos escogidos* in 1837, the year of Eugenio Hartzenbusch's *Los amantes de Teruel*; García Gutiérrez's *El trovador* was staged in 1836 and almost all of his poetry published by the mid-1840s; Rivas' *Romances históricos* appeared in 1841; Gil y Carrasco wrote every one of his thirty-seven poems between 1837 and 1847, even if his masterpiece novel *El Señor de Bembibre* did not appear until 1844; and between 1838 and 1843 Zorrilla had seen no less than sixteen of his plays put on stage plus several volumes of his poetry published. During the second and, without any doubt, most genuinely romantic period, we witness the mass return of political exiles from England, France and Italy following Fernando VII's death. The repatriation brought with it many of the reasons reflected in the success of Rivas' play.[9] The two absolutist repressions of 1814 and 1823 had sent abroad hundreds of intellectuals who could have given impetus to the new school of thought had they been allowed to act freely. Instead, those for whom Romanticism in literature meant liberalism in politics were forced to wait even longer before being allowed to put their ideals to the test. From exile they returned with clearer notions than those of their compatriots about European thought, politics, art, economics and literature. Their enthusiasm for a new order fomented the spread of *tertulias,* among the most important being the Ateneo, which remains today as Spain's most prestigious society of its kind and whose first president was the Duke of Rivas, and the Parnasillo, frequented as we know by Larra, Espronceda, Gil y Carrasco, Mesonero Romanos and Zorrilla.

The first two had died by the time Romanticism's most famous play, *Don Juan Tenorio* by Zorrilla, was staged in the Teatro de la Cruz on March 28, 1844, in Madrid. Zorrilla himself, though he continued to write until before his death in 1893, left Spain for France and then for Mexico when the Emperor Maximilian appointed him as director of that country's national theater. Gil y Carrasco died in 1846. The Duke of Rivas, increasingly involved with government service, published nothing after 1844. This year, then, is universally taken as the end of Spanish Romaticism. Both Gil y Carrasco's *El Señor de Bembibre,* also from 1844, and Zorrilla's *Don Juan*, justifiably famous, have nothing original about them. They constitute two catalogues of romantic themes, above all the latter—a mixture of prose and verse in a melodrama with total disregard for the three unities—protagonized by the donna-angelicata and the repentant sinner, ultimately joined and redeemed by love as the means of salvation. Romanticism's subsequent demise is evident. Not only did the number of works published later decline, but their force and originality also diminished noticeably. Only Zorrilla, constantly impoverished by bad management of his money—he had signed away his rights to the *Don Juan* for a pittance when he was twenty-six and then watched for fifty years as others became rich from its unending popularity—continued writing well into his seventies.

A movement thus characterized by its ephemeral—scarcely one decade—but intense existence faded from Spanish literature in 1844, notwithstanding the surfacing a quarter of a century later of Bécquer and Rosalia de Castro—Symbolists rather than true Romantics. Spanish Romanticism renewed the literary traditions of the eighteenth century. From the time of the Baroque poets Góngora and Quevedo, Spain waited well over one century to celebrate another handful of poets.[10] And while

Spanish Romanticism does not compare in either brilliance or longevity with the Golden Age period, having failed to produce universal works such as *Don Quijote*, true to its egocentric sentimental aesthetics, it resurrected one of literature's most memorable characters in Don Juan and achieved no small feat by initiating a lyrical and intimate subjetivism that engendered the modern verse we still enjoy today. Ironically, it was the daughter of Johan Böhl von Faber, remembered as Romanticism's earliest paladin, who under the pseudonym of Fernán Caballero ushered in the new literary era of Realism in Spain with her novel *La gaviota* published in 1849.

NOTES

1. Morse Peckham, «Toward a Theory of Romanticism,» *PMLA*, 66 (March 1961), 5-23.

2. *Ibid.*, p. 10.

3. *Ibid.*, p. 14.

4. F. Courtney Tarr, «Romanticism in Spain and Spanish Romanticism,» *Bulletin of Hispanic Studies*, 16 (1939), 39.

5. Edmund L. King, «What is Spanish Romanticism?,» *Studies in Romanticism*, 2 (Autumn 1962), 6.

6. *Ibid.*, p. 3.

7. Arthur O. Lovejoy, *Essays in the History of Ideas* (Baltimore, 1948), pp. 236-237.

8. Gabriel Lovett, *The Duke of Rivas* (Boston, 1977), p. 47.

9. Vicente Lloréns, *Liberales y románticos*, 2nd ed. (Madrid, 1968), pp. 383-385.

10. Pedro Salinas, *Ensayos de literatura hispánica* (Madrid, 1967), p. 273.

CHAPTER THREE

The First Poems

Although Espronceda wrote a number of long and undisputably superior poems in the second and last decade of his life as a poet compared to his first ten-year harvest, the first showings, nevertheless, because of their number, variety, briefness and historicity argue for a close look at them. Espronceda, beginning precociously at the age of fifteen with «Al 7 de julio,» had written over half of all his compositions by the time he was twenty-five years old. Not unexpectedly, the verses dating from 1822 until Espronceda had returned from exile to Spain in 1833 constitute for the most part a literary apprenticeship.

Generally viewed, these forty-some poems would not have gained any lasting laurels for Espronceda, and yet uppermost two considerations make their survey worthwhile. First, these compositions, though mostly unexciting and of little originality, are fertile soil for other later pieces, subsequently held as the most shining examples of Spanish Romanticism. Seminally, the themes of patriotism, dejected love, despair, and social excoriation are present from the very start in Espronceda's poetry. There is, as we shall see, a clearly discernable path travelled by the poet from the beginning to the end of his poetry, and the early poems point the critic in the right direction. Secondly, not all of the youthful verses deserve anonymous classification. Several, far from merely contributing to a poetic training, stand out as so many fine examples worthy of a more mature Espronceda. They can be found in nearly every thematic area the poet will touch in future years: «Fresca, lozana, pura y olorosa» dating from 1826-27 belongs to the amatory realm, «Himno al sol» of 1830-31 is in his best meditative vein, «A la muerte de Torrijos» of patriotic but historical significance dates from 1830, and «El Pelayo,» though a flawed epic composition, foreshadows Espronceda's ability to conceive a sustained poetical theme through hundreds of verses. Others equally meritorious will be examined in the pages that follow.

I. Classical and Neoclassical Influences

In June 1822 Madrid was a city wracked by violence. The King's guard, at constant odds with the populace who hated its indiscriminate firing into crowds demonstrating against Fernando VII's tyrannical rule, went one step further and, on the last day of June, shot one of its own more liberal officers. The ensuing protests were such in the country's largest city that for a week Madrid was paralyzed and the national guard had to be called to quell the rebellion. On July 7th they finally prevailed. Young Espronceda's first poetic composition commemorated the liberals' hour of glory in a most fitting format—an ode. Entitled, as mentioned above, «Al 7 de julio,» this poem now lost to us, nevertheless serves to underscore on the one hand Espronceda's unwavering socio-political involvement from his early youth and, on the other hand, his adeptness at choosing the appropriate poetic form for the occasion. The ode, from the time of the Greek Pindar (522-442 B.C.), has been universally used by poets to celebrate public events of a serious nature, eg. funerals, the unveiling of a memorial, the accession of a ruler to power, etc.

Under the tutelage of Alberto Lista, both at the school on San Mateo Street and the Academia del Mirto, Espronceda was first taught to admire the Latin classics, above all Horace. Espronceda mastered the Horacian ode, thus coinciding with the revival of this classical lyric from the other major romantics such as Shelley («Ode to the West Wind»), Keats («Ode to a Nightingale», «Ode to a Grecian Urn») and Tennyson («Ode on the Death of the Duke of Wellington»). His first efforts Espronceda unabashedly subtitled «Traducción de Horacio» and «Imitación de Horacio.» The former, «Vaticinio de Nereo,» a translation of ode fifteen from the first book of Horace, is an able rendering of the original wherein the Latin poet warns the brave young man who transports Helen of Troy in his boat of the fate that awaits them. As a nine-stanza *sexteto alirado* the poem has a formal style that conjures up the classic, slightly unreal quality of Greek and Latin myths. Neither its metaphors nor its tone distinguishes it from other available renditions of Horace's well-known poems.

The second composition «Vida del campo» lends itself to a more personal interpretation of the famous Horacian «Beatus ille . . .,» a veritable Nature *topos* in all poetry, at least since the Renaissance. Its ancestry in

Spanish poetry could not be more illustrious; Garcilaso, Herrera, Fray Luis, Quevedo, the Argensola brothers, Lope, and Góngora, to name but a few, all excelled in its composition. Fray Luis has three poems that echo Horace's moral pastoral, though his «Vida retirada»—sometimes called also «Vida del campo» just like Espronceda's—without a doubt remains the theme's masterpiece in all of Spanish literature. In Horace's poem, a city dweller escapes the corruption of the metropolis by moving to the country where he can live wisely and at peace. In Fray Luis', man flees the wickedness of urban life in search of a more placid and rewarding existence in the country that ultimately will lead him to God. Espronceda took this theme and presented a vision of the fortunate man who by dwelling in the country enjoys all of life's fruits. His reward is reaping, happy and untroubled, a plentiful harvest from his almost effortless work: he drinks wine from his own grapes, tastes savory apples in season, eats from the hunting of boar, deer and rabbit, tends to a flock of docile sheep, and rests under the shade of an oak tree lulled to sleep by the gentle warble of a nearby brook. Only in the two final stanzas do we confront reality—i.e., society—as the country dweller watching the ocean's high waves in the distance imagines the folly of those who would risk their lives crossing it in search of riches. This ending, significantly, recalls Fray Luis' own metaphor of merchants braving the sea—thus challenging it or, symbolically, Nature—and perishing for their covetousness.

Closer to Espronceda in time but equally distant from what would one day be his own uniquely romantic temper were the neoclassical poets Juan Meléndez Valdés and Alberto Lista. The latter's influence as his teacher and an able versifier is all too obvious in the compositions dated from 1821 to 1825 when Espronceda attended the San Mateo school. About this time we find also several other poems that recall Meléndez Valdés' artificial bucolic sentimentality. The «Romance a la mañana,» «La tormenta de noche,» and the sonnet «La noche» were found in the archives of the Academia del Mirto which Espronceda frequented while still a teenager. The last one follows closely the tone and content of Melénzez Valdés' ode, «De la noche,» from the first-person poetic persona and the frequent exclamatory notes in both to the sometimes identical expression: e.g. «lóbrego silencio» by Meléndez Valdés, «lúgubre silencio» by Espronceda.

In «La tormenta de noche» Espronceda again borrows from Meléndez Valdés the pastoral theme and the darkness setting, but the greatest debt there is owed to Lista whose «La tempestad» without question served as his model. Yet, aside from all of the *topoi,* the stereotyped neoclassical metaphors and the models followed, Espronceda did something completely new here that was to become a romantic trademark insofar as versification.

The poem, aptly subtitled «Idilio,» juxtaposes the theme of a raging storm with that of its defenseless victims (the shepherd in his shack, the protesting mother comforting her infant). This bifurcation of theme, however, carries over to the structure of the poem so that the longer, more violent verses depicting the tempest are contained in *silvas*, used to paint the plight of the helpless ones. Up to this point the combination of verses of differing meters had not been that uncommon in Spanish poetry though as far as the neoclassics—forever preoccupied with limits and perfectly balanced forms—were concerned, the ode, the sonnet, the tercet, the epic and the ballad occupied the highest places in their poetics. Espronceda, however, dared to combine not only individual unequal verses but also differing strophes, two in this case, the *octavilla* and the *silva*, in the same poem, thus beginning the metric innovations that by and large characterize romantic poetry.

II. Circumstantial Poetry: Panegyrics and Encomiums

The panegyric and the encomium are poems written in praise of men; the former dealing with the living and the second with the dead. Espronceda's first panegyric, not too surprisingly, was dedicated to his tutor Alberto Lista, who, having assumed the arcadian *nom de plume* Anfriso, received from the young poet the composition «A Anfriso en sus días.» Dated August 7, 1825, the sixteen-strophe ode carefully follows the classic mold, combining the occasional character of the Pindaric ode with the more reflective character of the Homeric one. In it, the poet celebrates emotionally Anfriso's own verses alluding to the most famous ones in clever ellipses that show Espronceda's thorough knowledge of Lista's poetry. From the seventh through the thirteenth stanzas, we find fourteen veiled references to his master's compositions. Elevated to that haven of immortal poets, Mount Parnassus, when crowned with laurels by Homer in the last strophe, Anfriso-Lista becomes the equal of Spain's great poets such as Herrera and Rioja also born in Seville, by the Betis (better known as the Guadalquivir) river, another of the poet's sycophants. Though its formal structure once again cannot be faulted and neither can the choice of metaphors and expected conventions, this panegyric reveals nothing new about its author. Espronceda's personality does not surface in any of its verses. Such is not quite the case in a latter *romancillo* also dedicated to Lista and titled «A Anfriso.» Devoid of the serious and exalted tone which characterized the earlier example, here Espronceda produces a flowing composition which, though steeped in the best neoclassic tradition of the eighteenth century, manages to convey a degree of emotion—the affection of a pupil for his teacher—with a touch of undisguised subjectivity—«pienso,» «vi»—absent until this moment.

The sincerity of emotion increased proportionately to the degree of the poet's involvement in the historical circumstance that engendered Espronceda's elegiac compositions. Thus, when writing the *romancillos* to his friend José García de Villalta or to Diego de Alvear y Ward on the death of his father, a deeper sentiment rings true in the poems. None of Espronceda's encomiums is more justly celebrated than his song «A la muerte de Don Joaquín de Pablo (Chapalangarra).» As will be recalled, Espronceda himself had been among that small group of volunteers who, under de Pablo's command, crossed the Pyrennees and invaded Spain through the Navarreese point of Valcarlos only to have their expedition cut short by a superior force of army regulars that also shot to death the legendary Chapalangarra. Since the ill-fated incursion into Fernando VII's Spain took place in October of 1830, the poem was probably written soon after that date, judging from the immediacy communicated by the first part of the piece. Relatively short, a mere sixty verses, it is divided into three parts: an introduction describing the poet himself and his surroundings in ballad form, an exordium by the foregoing figure in an *octava*, and a chorus of virgins and youths echoing his plaint. Part one, where two *cuartetos* bracket two more *octavas,* offers the most genuine verse of the whole composition. Foreshadowing the romantic importance that the poet himself was to assume as the subject of his own lyrics, Espronceda draws picture of an exiled young man who, perched atop the Pyrennees mountains surveys in grief not only his country's forbidden (to him) borders but also, below, the defeated remains of his leader and comrades who died trying to liberate Spain. The solitude of this mythical self-portrait and the sense of loss conveyed by the broken bodies left behind by the victorious royalist rabble are such that the reader feels witness to a scene of desolation. The central part, briefest of the three, is the voice of the poet who, overcome with emotion and for the moment powerless, cries out to the forces of justice, hope and revenge for help in avenging the slaughter of the hero and his men. And finally the closing segment, though within the realm of the classical song of lament for the dead, offers a most original and powerful metaphor which Góngora had used before and which Antonio Machado was to repeat after Espronceda—the image of the powerful man who, when falling, is likened to the strong oak wounded to death by the ax. Góngora's sonnet «De las muertes de Don Rodrigo Calderón, del Conde de Villamediana y Conde de Lemos» uses the symbol of a noble oak, while

Machado's «A un olmo seco» uses an elm.¹ But all three poets, with the same effect, depict the end of a noble being, once strong and now mowed down by fate. The funereal tone, perhaps a little too strident at the end of Espronceda's «A la muerte de Don Joaquín de Pablo (Chapalangarra),» is underscored by the youthful voices of the chorus which mourns Chapalangarra's death, much as the Greek choruses spoke eloquently on behalf of inexorable fate.

III. Epic Poetry

When Espronceda departed for the Saint Francis abbey in Guadalajara, condemned by the Spanish government on May 28, 1825, to spend five years in custody for having conspired against Fernando VII, the fifteen-year-old rebel took with him an outline for an epic poem. Lista had sketched out in detail for his disciple a plan for a twelve-canto epic dealing with the incipient stages of the Spanish Reconquest and its first leader Don Pelayo. As we now know Espronceda's confinement lasted only a few weeks, at most three months, consequently he did not complete the ambitious plan that Lista had envisioned for the work. Only half of the sections were composed, and these in a fragmentary and loosely tied fashion. Not until 1840, when twenty-one other poems and *El Estudiante de Salamanca* were published did the «Ensayo épico; Fragmentos de un poema titulado 'El Pelayo'» appear alongside them in public for the first time. In the intervening fifteen years Espronceda no doubt worked on the poem with the idea of finishing it. In March of 1828, while in exile in London, he asked his parents to forward him the incomplete poem so that he could show it to his friends there and make further progress on it. It seems unlikely that the request was ever heeded since, due to the exile's own unsavory reputation, when Fernando VII's police searched the elder Espronceda's house in Madrid the «Pelayo's» rough draft was listed among the briagadier's files and other documents. More plausible would be to assume that Espronceda worked on the poem, but never too diligently, after his return to Spain in 1833. Robert Marrast, basing his suppositions on intrinsic influences, has suggested that Espronceda may have added to the epic even before the 1833 date, as well as some more later up to 1835.²

Lista's carefully detailed outline, preserved thanks to Patricio de la Escosura, one of Espronceda's closest friends and editor of his 1884 *Obras poéticas y escritos en prosa,* was ordered thus:³

Canto primero: Pelayo va a Murcia a buscar auxilio para la guerra, en

Teodomiro. Recibimiento. Convite. Descripción del territorio del Segura. Adelinda, hija de Teodomiro.

Canto segundo: Narración de la batalla de Xerez, hecha por Pelayo, y de su navegación por las costas de Portugal.

Canto tercero: Consejo de los Demonios. Adelinda enamorada... declarar su amor... noble... Consejos de Ramiro.

Canto cuarto: Dios envía a Uriel, ángel de España, para que saque a Pelayo de su letargo. Noticia de lo que hacía García en Navarra.

Canto quinto: Despedida de Pelayo y desesperación de Adelinda...

Canto sexto: Asunto de Aldaimón. Navegación. Tempestad. Arribo a la Armórica. Guerra de aquella República contra el Duque de Bretaña.

Canto séptimo: Hazañas de Pelayo. Fin de la guerra y triunfo. Aldaimón... casarle con Adelinda.

Canto octavo: ...incite los españoles al Moncayo. El diablo de la luxuria apoderado de Munuza. Violación de Hormesinda.

Canto noveno: Pelayo vuelve: incita a sus paisanos: muerte de Munuza.

Canto décimo: Expedición de los moros contra los sublevados de Asturias. Combate de Alfonso con Hil...derín y narración de su vida.

Canto undécimo: Batalla de Covadonga.

Canto duodécimo: Toma de Gijón. Fundación de la Monarquía.

Aside from this basic plan, Lista also contributed sixty-one stanzas to the poem, of which only five were used, some modified and other untouched.' In all Espronceda wrote one hundred and twenty-four *octavas reales,* a most solemn strophe reserved for nobles and kings, made up of eight eleven-syllable verses with a consonantal rhyme of ABABABCC. Not only did Espronceda suppress most of Lista's stanzas, he also ignored almost completely his master's outline as we can see from the synopsis that follows. Divided the one hundred and twenty-nine *octavas reales* into six cantos, the poem's narrative sequence goes like this:

First canto: In the sumptuous court of Toledo, Don Rodrigo, the last Visigoth King, lays his eyes on the beautiful Florinda whereupon the skies turn dark in a pathetic fallacy foreshadowing disaster. (sixteen stanzas)

Second canto: In a dream sequence Don Rodrigo is threatened by Death armed with a scythe, he enjoys Florinda's company, and is awakened by her father, Count Julián, who struggles to choke him to death. (eight stanzas)

Third canto: In the longest segment of the poem Don Rodrigo and his men, in spite of his son Sancho's valiant efforts, are defeated and Spain falls into the hands of the infidel Moors. (fifty-eight stanzas)

Fourth canto: A portrayal of the magnificent Arabian capital city of

Córdoba, its king Alaimón and his plans for further conquest of Spanish territory. (twelve stanzas)

Fifth canto: A dual portrait of the riches and sensuous pleasures of Alaimón's court on the one side, and a vivid account of the privations and horrors of a besieged Spanish city on the other. (fifteen stanzas)

Sixth canto: In a night filled with thunder, the last of the Spanish resistors takes refuge in a church where Teudis, the old and feeble Sevillian leader, is comforted by Pelayo. Under Pelayo's commanding exhortations the remaining Spaniards regroup and succeed in breaking the Arab siege under cover of darkness. (twenty stanzas)

Pelayo, contrary to Lista's wishes as the epic's intended protagonist, does not appear by name until the seventh stanza of the last canto. Espronceda chose to start his poem prior to the beginning of the Reconquest and picked instead the demise of the Visigoth monarch Don Rodrigo, a more romantic figure who according to legend lost his throne and Spain as well in the course of his lascivious pursuit of Florinda, Count Julián's daughter. Her father's revenge for her rape by Rodrigo was to open Spain's southern gates to the hordes of Arab religious fanatics who followed Tarik and Muza across the straights of Gibraltar in a campaign they regarded as another holy war.

The «Pelayo» conforms to most traditional epics and by this criterion it must be judged; not on its originality because, even though the outline provided by Lista meant at most a point of departure for Espronceda, the poem offers no heuristic surprises. As Aristotle would have it, the action begins *in medias res*; it uses a single meter throughout, suited for a serious narrative; like Homer's *Iliad* and *Odyssey*, and Vergil's *Aeneid,* it deals with events in the distant past concerning noble and famous people of heroic deeds; nothing is invented, save for the occasional intercession of a *deus ex-machina* by the poet, since the actions of the hero as a historical figure are well known by everyone.

As a poetic exercise by Espronceda, then, the «Pelayo» is a very successful undertaking, especially when one remembers that its author was barely seventeen years of age when he wrote most, if not all of it. Uniquely Espronceda's at this stage are the themes of revenge, vice, decadent love, dreams, and privation; the scenes of action, darkness and splendor; the use of the rhetorical figures antithesis, hyperbaton and prosopopeia;[5] and the narrative perspective given over to the protagonist in the third and sixth cantos. The poet is burdened from the very beginning by a ponderous theme, an obligatory versification totally cumbersome, and a corresponding litany of metaphors and abused expressions. In spite of it all, Espronceda managed to dispel much of the not unexpected rigidity and bookish unoriginality by injecting believeable, if flawed, passions into many of the characters and by alternating violence, sentimentality, decadence and historicity in the cantos. Moreover, the sustained poetical effort giving forth a one-thousand verse poem augured well for the creator of *El Estudiante de Salamanca* and *El Diablo Mundo*.

IV. Patriotic Exile Songs

In the ten-year period between 1823 and 1833 over one thousand liberal Spaniards sought political asylum in London and about twice the same number fled to Paris. There were still others, perhaps five hundred or so, who found in other European countries, Belgium, Italy, Portugal and even in Morocco, a more hospitable place for their ideas than their own nation offered them.[6] These were military men, lawyers, priests, men of letters and other professionals opposed to the absolutist government of Fernando VII. The youngest of the Spanish emigrés in London was José de Espronceda,[7] who, as we already know, arrived there on September 15, 1827, and remained until February 28, 1829, at which point he left for Paris, though he returned again to England on February 21, 1832, staying this last time until August 1 of the same year. In all, Espronceda's exile, forced like all others by Fernando VII's despotic rule as well as by his own indomitable spirit of adventure, lasted approximately six years. During this time when he was pretty much on his own, Espronceda received financial help from his father and at the same time from the British and, in turn, the French governments. Learning to cope by himself he also derived an additional income from the fencing lessons he gave. Little else is known of his stay in England except it must have been much more tranquil than the months spent in France where his involvement in conspiracies, rebellions and protests of every sort has been mentioned. He, of course, had Teresa to think about, but like all displaced political men, Espronceda's mind and heart were never very far from his country. He wrote over twenty poems during those six years, most of this labor taking place in London where there was little chance for action other than the plotting in which expatriates customarily engage themselves.

Banished from Spain, Espronceda thought seriously of little else as we can see by three poems which punctuate his existence abroad: «La entrada del invierno en Londres» 1828, «A la Patria» 1829, and «A la muerte de Torrijos y sus compañeros» 1830.

Dedicated to his friend and fellow exile, Balbino Cortés, who then published it in 1846 after Espronceda's death, the thirteen-*silva* stanzas that make up «La entrada del invierno en Londres» should be understood on two levels. A first one (v. 1-12, 13-48, 61-84), penned in a mournful and melancholy tone, decries the harshness of winter that permeates the exiled poet's spirit as opposed to the comfort found by the shepherd in his cabin, the wise man in the calm of his thoughts, the sailor safe in port, or even the patriot who never had to leave his homeland. On a second level (v. 49-60, 85-156), the tenor, free from the neoclassic *topoi* mentioned above, is established by the poet's most intimate sense of loss at being exiled from his country. In these later verses Espronceda's sadness, made more acute by the winter's cold and desolate character, manifests itself in an unburdening of emotions: the loss of his own and his country's freedom, his separation from it, Spain's improverishment and his fervent desire to return. The exile's moving feelings reveal a sentimental and personal sincerity heretofore absent from Espronceda's verses of this nature, where the subject had not been soley the poet himself. In spite of a vague neoclassic prop here and there, the inspiration is recognizably Espronceda's as are some of images: «Bajel dichoso», «tu vela en popa hinchando/ el aligero viento . . .», later seen in «La canción del pirata.»

Again making use of the eleven- and seven-syllable lines alternately arranged in quartets, Espronceda wrote «A la Patria,» perhaps the finest of his patriotic verses. It is an elegy to lost freedom, surveying Spain's history from the time of the Hapsburg Phillip II, «la nación cuyo imperio se extendía/ del Ocaso al Oriente!» until the date of the poem's composition when the nation had fallen «so la rabia . . ./ del déspota sombrío» Fernando VII. The underlying theme is that of *ubi sunt:* where have the glory, the heroes, the fame, the power, the riches that were Spain's gone?

> Un tiempo España fue; cien héroes fueron
> en tiempos de ventura,
> y las naciones tímidas la vieron
> vistosa en hermosura. (v. 45-49)

The whole length of the seventeen strophes is dominated by the comparison of the *then* and the *now,* underscoring the declining Spain who, separated from her best men by either their deaths or their banishment, had not one left to rescue her from the ravages of the tyrant. The poet's hurt at helplessly watching from afar the inexorable destruction of his country is expressed nevertheless in contained, at times majestic, tones which raise the lament to the level of a vision as inspiring as Quevedo's Golden Age masterpiece «Miré los muros de la patria mía». That Espronceda knew

Quevedo's sonnet there can be no doubt when both poems stand side by side. First Quevedo's, then Espronceda's:

> Miré los muros de la patria mía,
> Si en un tiempo fuertes, ya desmoronados,
> de larga edad y de vejez cargados
> dando obediencia al tiempo en muerte fría
>
> (v. 1-4)
>
> ....
>
> Entré en mi casa, y vi que, descansada
> se entregaba a los años por despojos:
> sale mi espada la misma suerte. (v. 9-11)

* * *

> ¿Qué se hicieron tus muros torreados?
> ¡Oh mi patria querida!
> ¿Dónde fueron tus héroes esforzados,
> tu espada no vencida? (v. 37-40)

Espronceda may have not caught the full meaning of Quevedo's psalm since the baroque poet addresses himself more to the imminence of death than to the decline of his country. Bruce W. Wardropper suggests that «the crumbling walls of the poet's native town (*patria*) symbolize the flight of time. . . The poet's tumbledown house probably is an image of his aging body. The sword is drawn in token of surrender.»[8] And yet Espronceda, here a creature within his own creation, conveys a feeling of equal grief at seeing the nation of which he feels a consanguineous part—«sus hijos implorando»—being destroyed by a cruel master.

Espronceda's liberalism drove him to loathe Fernando VII against whom he had fought in Spain and afterwards from exile. Patriotism and freedom were two concepts in which he firmly believed and which for him became one at the beginning of his adult life while abroad. Inspired by campaigns and liberal figures, Espronceda wrote many political poems up to his final days as his last sonnet «A Guardia» demonstrates. Many of these poems due to their circumstantial and intranscendent nature can be forgotten. Espronceda's Romanticism, as was the case with his fellow Romantics', was largely a protest movement, where no plan was offered nor plans put forth that could substitute for the values they all proferred to disdain. Romanticism became a revolution of a negative sign, a final acceptance—emotional, not intellectual—of the discredit pronounced by the

French *philosophes* of the *Encyclopedie* of all the old values.

The sonnet «A la muerte de Torrijos y sus compañeros» best synthesizes Espronceda's hate of the King Fernando VII, his love for those who die martyrs in a struggle against the oppressor, and his own impotent anger. Espronceda succeeds in elevating a historical footnote into a universal paradigm of the human condition—man's valiant if at times futile struggle in the face of threatening social and spiritual slavery. Field marshall José María de Torrijos and his fifty-two men, among them the Englishman Robert Boyd, landed in the port city of Fuengirola on December 4, 1831, but the Governor of Málaga, in whom they had confided in order to carry out their mission, betrayed them to the royal spy network. Captured by the king's chief of police they were all summarily executed. In spite of a complete dearth of names and dates in this sonnet, the fate of these patriots cannot be easily forgotten by any man as convinced as Espronceda was that life in a nation without freedom must be put on the line to unseat the enslaving tyrant.

V. Influences in Exile: Ossian, Scott, Byron

Toward the end of his exile, in the early 1830s, Espronceda began taking notice of the poetry of the Gaelic bard Ossian (3 A.D.) that James Macpherson had published from 1760-1765.⁹ Ostensibly Macpherson served only as an editor for Ossian, though there is reason to suspect that many of the poems he passed off as originals were actually his, mere imitations of early Gaelic poetry. The impact of the Ossianic poems in English literature is slight but in Europe was disproportionately vaster than their intrinsic worth merits. Goethe's own *Werther* betrays the overblown importance this apocryphal verse had even on great minds. Napoleon Bonaparte is said to have taken Macpherson's edition of the *Ossianic Poems* to St. Helena with him.

Espronceda may have been acquainted with Ossian at the time he studied with Lista but not until his «A la muerte de Don Joaquín de Pablo (Chapalangarra)» do we detect any sign of Ossianism. No doubt what Espronceda found attrative in this new old mode were the motifs that read like a catalog for Romanticism: the raging north winds, the pale moonlight rays, sepulchral settings, dark and fast moving clouds, deep still-water lakes, a pervasive and melancholy Nature. The first part of «A la muerte de Don Joaquín de Pablo (Chapalangarra),» described previously as a ballad form (v. 1-28), where the poet introduces himself and describes the surroundings, clearly belongs to the Ossianic mode. Portrayed as a disconsolate young warrior lamenting the loss of his fellow combatants, the poet, broken sword at his side, defiantly withstands alone the forces of a raging storm at the top of the Pyrennees, exhorting men and gods to avenge the deaths of the fallen.

The most characteristic poem of this series, if not the best, is the two part «Oscar y Malvina. Imitación del estilo de Osián. A tale of times of old.» Oscar, the son of Ossian, going off to war says goodbye to his wife Malvina, the daughter of Toscar, king of Ulster, in part one titled «La despedida.» The longest of the two, this initial section lacks movement and action. In descriptive scene settings, Espronceda draws from Ossian's best known works, *Cath-Loda, Carthon, Temora,* and *Fingal,* recreating the legends and motifs of the bard. Thus, we find the lovers in the landscape of Mount Morven, with its perennial snows and the deep surrounding valleys, listening to the echo of Ossian's voice, while the moonlight breaks through the mists as they look up in silence to Fingal's (King of Morven) ruinous ivy-covered fortress. As the wind carries their names through the night, Malvina, pure but passionate, weeps as Oscar departs, his armor shining in the moonlight and barely audible through the forest. The second part, «El combate,» though according to Macpherson[10] had taken place during one of the feasts of shells of ancient tradition at Cairbar's palace, in Espronceda's poem happens in a clearing of the woods where Cairbar, usurper of the throne of Ireland and murderer of Ossian's grandfather, sleeps by a smoldering fire. Barely nine stanzas long (v. 108-169), here we see Oscar's noble character as he awakens Cairbar and challenges him to a duel which in a titanic fashion has thunder, lightning and raging winds as the backdrop. Though action substitutes for description, it is largely narrative. The dialogue, cut when barely begun and excised by dotted lines, does not go beyond the Ossianic cliches. The ending, too, follows the Macpherson pattern as both warriors die at each other's hands with the coming of dawn.

While by no means original, «Oscar and Malvina» is not a mere copy or simple translation of Ossian. Espronceda, inspired by the appeal of this exotic and legendary world, its personnages, ambient and emotions, assimilated it sufficiently to fashion his own Ossianic compositions probably much in the same way James Macpherson himself did. Much of what he learned from Ossian, whether through Macpherson, Byron or even the first Spaniards to translate him (José Alonso Ortiz, Marchena, Pedro Montegón), Espronceda retained and later made his own as a true Romantic: e.g., night scenes, the *donna angelicata*, the fierce storms, the impossi-

ble love depicted in the farewell, the lyric sentimentality, the play of opposites, and a great deal of the vocabulary.

Among those caught up in the Ossianic revival trend, the address to
the stars and the planets became something of a must. Of course Horace,
among the Augustan Latin poets, had also used the sun as an object to be
revered, as had Fray Luis and, closer to Espronceda, Cienfuegos, Quintana, Jovellanos, Meléndez Valdés, Lista and José María de Heredia. In
fact, the last four all wrote compositions titled «Al sol,» the same name
Espronceda gave to this. The Ossianic address to the sun in *Carthon*, furthermore, has its Spanish translator in José Marchena,[11] and Lord Byron
treated the same incident in his *Manfred*. Who can doubt that Espronceda
knew at least some if not all of these works?

It shares with these compositions the well-worn neoclassic conventions
learned from Lista's ample classics reading lists: the praise to the most
refulgent star in the universe, the expected hyperboles, the grandiloquence
of the language, the fountain-of-life motif, the use of a long meter—the
silva with its slow hendecasyllabic cadence alternating with heptasyllabic
verses. Within this rigid framework, however, Espronceda did something
remarkably refreshing by turning the hymn, as he subtitled it, into a mock-
ing discourse which brings the sun down to less than immortal level. The
poem can be best appreciated if divided into three sections according to the
tone and content of each.

The initial piece (v. 1-78), also the most extensive, contains the saluta-
tion in direct address form to the sun, playing on the glorifying formulae
listed above with some of Espronceda's own additions, eg. the poet's sense
of wonder, as a child, at the sun's brightness and its majestic path through
the heavens. Less original are the references to the sun's immunity to the
passing of time, its invulnerability from cataclysms such as the Flood, its
indifference to wars among kings, and its immutability in the space it oc-
cupies in the universe. Yet, even here Espronceda has been laying the
groundwork for the powerful star's undoing. He accomplishes it by affir-
mations wondrous beyound belief, a series of litotes so hyperbolic as to cast
doubt on their reality. For, how can the sun be beyond divine reach—«libre
tú de la cólera divina»—without being a god—«tú, como Señor del
mundo,/ sobre la tempestad tu tronzo alzabas»—who takes unto himself
the property of eternal? It is at this point that the quasideification stops
suddenly and the poem heads in another direction.

Part two (v. 79-92) is a single strophe that begins and ends with a question mark. «Just what makes you better than, or even different from, the
rest of mortal beings in this universe which itself is likely doomed to disappear someday?» Espronceda begins with an erotesis to the sun. Even as the

ruler of our firmament, which the poet admits the sun personifies, it too ultimately will fall prey to Death's scythe. It will take longer than for the rest of men but Death will have her way in the end since there exists always a greater and more powerful entity than ourselves. And here, in the last quatrain of the eighth stanza

> ¿Quién sabe si tal vez pobre destello
> eres tú de otro sol que otro universo
> mayor que el nuestro un día
> con doble resplandor esclarecía (v. 89-92)

Espronceda finally reveals the key of this about-face to be a sense of cosmic jealousy. As man, though made in the image of his creator, is fated to die, why should the sun, likely a reflection of his own maker, be spared a different end? If man is to perish, Espronceda cannot be satisfied unless the sun too disappears.

Consequently, the final segment, also only one stanza in length (v. 93-106), further identifies the sun with man and subjects it to the same divine law which determines our destiny. Its central *topos*, the oldest and most enduring in literature, applies equally to man and sun. It is the theme of the *carpe diem*, seize the day—«Goza tu juventud y tu hermosura, / ¿Oh sol!. . .» —because the brevity of life and the finality of death cannot be escaped or even altered once God decides that the time has come. Ironically, the sun's demise, as Espronceda would have it, will be so total that no trace will be left behind.

> en tinieblas sin fin tu llama pura
> entonces morirá. Noche sombría
> cubrirá eterna la celeste cumbre;
> ni aun quedará reliquia de tu lumbre. (v. 103-106)

The sun that is greater than man, more powerful, lives longer and higher, shines brighter, will one day vanish more totally than man for whom the «relic» of the final line seems to be reserved. The prefixes *des*- and *dis*-, meaning «un-,» which Espronceda had used in the first part of the poem to underscore mortal man's short existence—*desplomarse, disiparse, desprendidas, desaparecen, desvanecerse*— now apply, with a force equally determined to undermine, to the sun in these last verses (v. 98, 99): *descienda, deshecho, destrozado*.

The poet has had his say and broken with all tradition in this malevolent address to the sun, ostensibly composed in its honor.

Espronceda at this juncture began his independent journey as a romantic poet, having graduated from bibliographical inspiration to more personal poetic dictates. The inconformity with life as he was forced to live it drove him deeper into rebelliousness, metaphysically, socially and at the end stopped short of turning on himself by espousing the narcissism so evident in the «Canto a Teresa.» The process closely corresponds to the toppling, outlined in Chapter Two, of the static metaphysical structure of the Classics that gave way to the new dynamic organicism, for a time disorienting to so many of the Romantics. Espronceda, not unlike them, was ready to discard the old irreverently if need be as we saw in «Al Sol.» How could he accept the epicenter of the universe as perfect and everlasting if the universe, growing and thus changing, was no longer considered perfect? Espronceda de-mythified the sun by bringing it down to man's miserable level even if its destruction meant his own as well.

VI. The First Love Poems

Up until 1951 everyone—writers, publishers, editors—accepted as Espronceda's own the poem «Despedida del patriota griego de la hija del apóstata,» since neither the poet nor his contemporaries pointed out differently, and in the past Espronceda had been quick to acknowledge his direct or inspirational indebtedness to Horace, Ossian, Lista and others. The fact is, however, that, as Vicente Lloréns discovered,[12] Espronceda's theretofore «original» poem turned out to be a translation from English of the anonymous composition «The Patriot and the Apostate's Daughter, or the Greek Lover's Farewell,» which had appeared in 1824 in the *New Monthly Magazine and Literary Journal* of London. This journal, edited by Thomas Campbell at this time, was well known by the Spaniard exiles for it celebrated their cause and published numerous pieces about Spain, its history, art and literature, some of which were written by Spaniards themselves.

The original poem, a lyric composition of 108 consonantal verses, was rendered by Espronceda as a 134 line *romance heroico* with its characteristic eleven-syllable verses of an assonantal rhyme and its predominately narrative scheme. For all of these changes, however, the two poems read as one, and scholars may be forgiven for having attributed it to the Spaniard for over a century. «Despedida del patriota griego de la hija del apóstata,» save for the Hellenistic and specifically religious themes, is a showcase of Esproncedian motifs, past and future. He may not have fathered the poem's main themes, but he certainly recognized them as identical to his own deeply felt ones. Consequently Espronceda's Spanish version is totally faithful to the English one.

The lover's sorrowful parting, the rebellion against tyranny, the prejudiced alternative between friends and death, the inescapability of adverse fate, the nostalgia for the past and the veiled hope in the future, and the patriotic sacrifice of one's life are all motifs which pertain to Espronceda's life as well as his poetry. That he found them in someone else's poem must have moved him to write his own version of the work, with the result that though the Spanish one interprets, expands and rearranges, its fidelity to the English model is completely understandable and consequent with Espronceda's ideals and sentiments. It represents also the first time that a love poem and a patriotic song—this poet's life coordinates—are perfectly integrated into one masterful composition.

Although the topic of lovers' unhappy farewells had been seen in earlier poems (e.g. «Oscar y Malvina») and would play a great role in future ones (e.g. «Canto a Teresa»), we can find a small gathering of verse where love's triumph constitutes the salient feelings perhaps for the first and last time in all of Espronceda's poetry. By the time Espronceda wrote «A un ruiseñor» he had already produced five earlier sonnets: an untitled one, «La noche,» «A Eva,» «Rosas y esperanzas» and «A la muerte de Torrijos y sus compañeros.» The date of the composition for «A un ruiseñor,» judging from intrinsic evidence, was assumed to be 1832 by Robert Marrast,[13] which means that Espronceda was to write only three more sonnets during the rest of his life, one of which, «A una mariposa,» will be discussed shortly.

«A un ruiseñor» retains the traditional Petrarchan sonnet's rhyme scheme of ABBA ABBA CDE CDE but the pertinent division of meaning expected between the two quatrains and the two tercets does not materialize. Espronceda instead chose as the poem's first cluster not only the two quatrains but also the first tercet and the inaugural line of the second one. This, remarkably similar to the Spenserian (ABAB BCBC CDCD EE) and Shakesperian (ABABA CDCD EFEF GG) models of the English Renaissance arranged in three quatrains and one final couplet, is no doubt a result of Espronceda's readings while in London coinciding with the early 1830s date of the poem's composition. Espronceda, thus, retained the structure but shifted the correspondence of meaning, eschewing the expected expositional content of the quatrains and the conclusive nature of the tercets characteristic of the Italian model.

The turning point of the sonnet «A un ruiseñor» is to be found in the initial word of the thirteenth verse (second line of the last tercet), *cual,* («as»). The comparative «as» bifurcates the poem into a dilated simile. In its first part we learn of the sad love songs of the nightingale whose lament is shared in serialized pathetic fallacies by the pearls of dawn (early morning dew), a rose colored sky, a sighing evening breeze through compassionate woods, and the night stillness presided over by a silent moon—a complete cycle from morning until night. All of these manifestations of Nature echo the bird's sadness. And yet the sweetness of its song is such that the poet's own melancholy finds relief in its sound: «Cual bálsamo süave en mis pesares, / endulzará tu acento el llanto mío.» The poet, appearing personally for the first time in these last two verses of the sonnet comprising its conclusive meaning, finds solace in the fellowship felt with another's love cares. Though «A un ruiseñor» does not celebrate the joys of love, it dwells lovingly on the joy of the uncertainties and plaints of the lover who, nevertheless, feels that his passion cannot go unrewarded endlessly.

«A una mariposa,» the last sonnet that Espronceda wrote for almost another decade,[14] stands as one of his happiest love poems. In it he essays a second often-used rhyme scheme of the tercets in the Spanish sonnet, CDC DCD, contrasting with the previous CDE CDE seen in «A un ruiseñor.» Equally different from the earler composition is the absence of a marked break in the internal structure as the transition from the second quatrain to the first tercet takes place. Only a progression to a more personalized attitude on the part of the poet can be detected. The butterfly, an observable symbol of love's innocence in the quatrains, serves as the lover's messenger in the tercets. It functions thusly as a link between the strophes, fluttering from flower to flower delicately seeking their sweet perfume until the lover points to the softest most fragrant flower: the lips of the beloved. That is the flower he beseeches the butterfly to kiss on his behalf. Punctuated by three only metaphors (the butterfly first as a speck of light, and then as an image of love's purity; the mouth of the beloved woman as a flower), the light rhythm of the poem flows easily and recalls the restless skipping of the colorful butterfly among the springtime blossoms. The tone of the young love established by the nascent season, the happiness symbolized by the bright colors, and the beauty conjured up by the fresh lips of the beloved seldom attain the exuberant joy contained in this early sonnet.

Dating from the same period (1823-33) when Espronceda and Teresa began living together[15] are two more love lyrics, both untitled, that sing the happiness of a love shared at last. «Y a la luz del crepúsculo serena...» begins the three-*octava* poem. Here the relatively long verses establish *a priori* its dominant tranquil note further underscored by the intimacy of a calm night, by the vaguely satisfied lover in the presence of his beloved, and by the timelessness in which both now dwell signified by the copulative conjunction *y* that not only introduces the three separate stanzas but which recurs ten times throughout the poem. Though not lacking in emotion, the two first strophes are characteristically prefatory. The opening one sets the stage and the mood: a deserted beach at dusk where the moon on a distant horizon illuminates a picture of waves calmly lapping at the sand. In the next *octava* love's presence is felt in a progressively more intense manner by an awakening from dreams about the beloved now realized by her immediacy. The poem climaxes in its third stanza where the passion felt by the lovers in this sensual lyric completely dominates. Overcome with each other's presence, the poem ends short of an erotic consummation as the lover succumbs yearningly «...al beso y al placer /que/ provoca/ con dulce anhelo la entreabierta boca.» A comparable sensuality reappeared a few years later in the poem « A Jarifa en una orgía,» though the fervor and the passionate anticipation are jaded and no longer blind the lover to life's pitfalls.

Not too dissimilar in theme, tone and structure to the above composition is the poem beginning with the declarative «Suave es tu sonrisa, amada mía» which remained unpublished until 1907.[14] Three irregular strophes of seven verses each, vaguely resembling a *lira* (normally a five-line stanza of eleven- and seven-syllable verses consonantally rhyming aBabB, but which here is a combination of seven eleven- and seven-syllable verses where the first rhymes consonantally with the third, the sixth with the seventh, and the rest are blank) divulge a less carnal though no less intense relationship. The woman, more than an object of love, is an object of worship, «Tú mi divinidad; yo a ti rendido, / extático en tu faz miro el cielo,» says the poet in verses 9-10, and concludes the stanza declaring «pagado en amor feliz te adoro.» Her ethereal quality first noted in the softness of her smile (v. 1), then in her comparison to a placid moonbeam (v. 4), and finally in the tenderness with which the lover seeks to adore her (v. 13-34), hint at the indissoluble duality passion-purity endemic to every romantic heroine.

Whereas in the first two stanzas the woman had been both the subject and the object of the poet's declamations as the initial verse of the poem («Suave es tu sonrisa...») and the first line of the second strophe («Tu /eres/ mi divinidad...») attest, the last stanza is wholly taken over by the lover's ardor: «Yo enjugo el llanto...», «Yo en alegría...», «Yo en tus labios...». The tenderness of the emotion, attenuated by a love which is half worship, demands only a kiss in order to be satiated rather than as a prelude to a more sensual resolution.

Though caution must be taken to avoid direct correlation between the poet's biography and his literary creations («intentional fallacy»), there can be little doubt in the case of these four poems dating from 1832 to 1833 that at least their inspiration had much to do with the happiness found by Espronceda in being together with Teresa, his greatest and most lasting love.[17] Its sentimental implications crystalized nowhere else in Espronceda's poetry as gently and ideally as in these love poems.

NOTES

1. Richard López Landeira, «Machado en su poema: 'A un olmo seco',» *Modern Language Notes,* 86 (March 1971), 280-84.

2. *Poesías líricas y fragmentos épicos,* Robert Marrast, ed., p. 29.

3. *Ibid.,* pp. 291-93.

4. *Ibid.,* p. 28.

5. Domingo Ynduráin, *Análisis formal de la poesía de Espronceda* (Madrid, 1971), pp. 25-168.

6. Vicente Lloréns, *Liberales y románticos,* 2nd edition (Madrid, 1968), pp. 23-46.

7. *Ibid.,* p. 36.

8. Bruce W. Wardropper, *Spanish Poetry of the Golden Age* (New York, 1971), p. 30.

9. Joaquín Casalduero, *Espronceda* (Madrid, 1967), p. 124.

10. *Ibid.,* p. 129.

11. Edgar Allison Peers, «The Influence of Ossian in Spain,» *Philological Quarterly,* 6 (1925), 133-35.

12. Vicente Lloréns, «El original inglés de una poesía de Espronceda,» *Nueva Revista de Filología Hispánica,* 5 (1951), 418-22.

13. Robert Marrast, *José de Espronceda et son temps* (Paris, 1974), p. 212.

14. *Ibid.,* p. 199.

15. *Ibid.,* p. 213.

16. *Poesías líricas y fragmentos épicos,* Robert Marrast, ed., p. 200.

17. Robert Marrast, *José de Espronceda et son temps* (Paris, 1974), p. 213.

CHAPTER FOUR

Social and Political Poetry

The elegy to lost freedom seen earlier in Chapter Three in the poem «A la patria» voiced the poet's most enduring ideal, the pursuit of freedom in patriotic terms. Manifested as a historical rendering that universalizes Espronceda's protests against Fernando VII's tyrannical rule, «A la patria» would give way some five years later to a cycle of poems that are the culmination of his belief in man's need for complete liberty.

I. Five Songs

The series known collectively as the «Canciones» represents the most notable stage of Espronceda's lyric of thought.[1] Derived from a purely personal inspiration, the poet takes on for the first and only time the mission of reformer which, as a Romantic, he always pretended to carry out, producing a poetry characterized by a violent exaltation of himself together with an equally fervent cry for limitless freedom. The largely anonymous collectivism observed in «A la patria» and its political patriotism here turn into an intensely subjective expression on the part of the poet and into an attitude of social protest altogether nonconformist. From the national entity Espronceda went to the individual citizen and from patriotic concerns he moved to social preoccupations. In the «Canciones» the attack is directed against the society on two fronts: civil liberty and moral freedom. Both proclaim an ethical end where man's liberty can be contemplated as the ultimate aspiration in opposition to any sort of social sanction. The persuasiveness of these two freedoms with their vituperation against a civilized society, basically unjust and selfish, is wielded as a weapon on behalf of man's right to total independence. In Espronceda's view, shared by other

Romantics, man can come very close to a harmonious existence with the solitude reflected in the universe, but he is denied an equally peaceful social coexistence. He is alone on one side facing the rest of the world on an opposing side.[2]

Had Espronceda written solely the five «Canciones» his fame would have hardly been less than what it is today. Save for one, «El canto del cosaco,» this group of poems inaugurates a poetic tradition in Spanish literature[3] not only on account of their polymetric schemata, which is sonorous, sweeping and remarkably unadorned, but also because of their nature as poésie engagée. «El canto del cosaco,» as a result of its traditional quatrain structure and a largely conventional idiom—romantically tiresome in theme and tone—, falls short of the inspiration of the «Canción del pirata,» «El mendigo,» «El verdugo» and «El reo de muerte.» The last four, moreover, were all written within one year of each other, between 1834 and 1835, whereas the first one did not appear until approximately four years later. The rapid elaboration of these four can be ascribed to a unity of conception and realization, an uncharacteristic urgency in Espronceda who seldom hurried his verse either because he preferred the real to the poetic circumstance or else because the task of perfecting his work concerned him more than most critics have been willing to admit.

Each of the «Canciones» extols one only personnage whose life the poet employs to sketch a stylized portrait of the slavery, misery, oppression and cruelty inflicted by society on the individual. «Canción del pirata,» «El mendigo» and «El verdugo» are all done from the first person point of view. In the case of the first two characters, both succeed in dodging the social yoke by means of their self-alienation. On the other hand, the executioner and the condemned man are victims of society and repositories of their hatred. Given the poet's rebellious temper, the figures of the pirate and the beggar are a cut above the other two anti-heroes. The arrogant vain-glory of the first two that has made them victorious in a hostile environment plays opposite a sentiment of deception and bitterness in the other two. Espronceda applauds the sovereignty of the pirate and the independence of the beggar because symbolically they personify the individual who can prevail against society, whereas the executioner and the condemned are to be pitied in their impotence to overcome an ill fate. The idealizing of these four misfits, contrasted with an amorphous society viewed negatively, constitutes the paradox of the continuing skepticism begun with the Enlightment and a discontinuation resulting from Espronceda's inability to withstand the separation from a remote past. I refer here not only to the past of a medieval Spain, akin to García Gutiérrez' but to the

Spain of mendicants, executioners, criminals and, later, to virginal *donne angelicate* as well.

II. The Pirate and the Beggarman

The «Canción del pirata,» cornerstone of Spanish romantic poetry, exhibits, like no other poem of Espronceda, the need for and the enjoyment of individual liberty to the detriment of society. Repeated five times, the second verse of the ritornello, «Que es mi Dios la libertad», serves as the constant reminder in the life of an outlaw always in peril of losing his head. On another count, the ritornello alone would have been sufficiently scandalous even for the most lukewarm Catholic reader of the nineteenth century. There exists an implicit blasphemy in these verses, the equivalent of saying «I have no God other than my own will»—a denial as political as it is moral. It is too apparent that life and freedom are indivisible since the enjoyment of the latter derives from having suffered under an oppressive society as these verses affirm: «Cuando el yugo/ del esclavo,/ como un bravo/ sacudí.» In other words, to lose one's freedom means to lose one's life. The pirate willingly gambles his own, feeling superior to the rest of mankind which he considers a mortal enemy. The pirate's disdainful attitude toward life only applies when his existence cannot be determined by an autonomous choice, free from the bonds embodied in man-made and even divine laws, since he has Liberty as his only god. Contrary to the outlaw who may flee in order to escape punishment but who gladly would return to the midst of society were his crime to be pardoned, the pirate rejects such a choice because for him social co-existence, even as an exonerated man, is the equivalent of a mutiliated existence. The «Canción del pirata» is perhaps the most romantic of the «Canciones» and, by all appearances, the least social of the five. The poem seems to be a freedom cry for the benefit of an adventurer, though empty of intentional harm against anyone else. At most it could be interpreted as an expression of defiance against society, possibly the world, but so far without any specific condemnation implied. Nevertheless, the pirate clearly harms his fellowman, patently those he takes hostage and to a lesser degree to the victim's dependents. Here the paradox of Romanticism can be seen quite clearly. It is the never ending contradiction between the sought-after ideal and the price of attaining such a longing. When Espronceda celebrates his god, Freedom, someone somewhere has to be offered up in sacrifice.

A similar note of admiration expressed by Espronceda toward the pirate sounds again in «El mendigo,» a poem which structurally is the twin of the one discussed above. Both are constructed upon rigid polymetric structures of ninety and one hundred and eighteen lines respectively, arranged in similar patterns of introductory and narrative stanzas interspersed with ritornellos and concluding refrains. The verse length ranges from the *verso quebrado* of four syllables to the longer hendecasyllabic *cuarteto*, a variety that accomodates the internal pace of the poem where direct speech, narration, action and recapitulation all demand differing rhythms.

In the poem «El mendigo» the individual lives in society's midst, at least it so appears; the pirate, on the other hand was physically as well as spiritually far removed from civilization. However, the beggar's internal attitude reveals the scorn he feels for his society. He lives off of it, hypocritically shielding himself behind the fear that others have of God—a Being whose very existence he denies. The beggar is a beguiler who mocks his benefactors as much as those who loathe him, boastful of his wretchedness in a singular reversal of values. Without a god, friendships, needs, possessions or any belief with which to sustain him other than a perverse cynicism, the beggar is a confirmed nihilist. He can be found at the opposite extreme of the pirate's defiant haughtiness. The pirate proclaimed his freedom openly, whereas the beggar parodies him in an iniquitous and underhanded manner. Espronceda portrays a man who lives off of society but not in it; outside of society but a parasite indebted to it.

The beggar inverts social values using them as a two-edged sword to defeat society on its own terrain. The sanction here is clearly worthy of the picaresque genre. Certainly the beggar, insofar as he lives by his wits to outsmart society so that he can eat without working, is a real *pícaro*, although it would be equally valid to look upon his lack of appetites of any kind as suggesting a perverse stoicism. The condemnation drawn by Espronceda is astonishing because if the social classes that succor the beggar do so exclusively out of a fear of God from their comfortable state, they can only be held in contempt, whereas the beggar is to be spurned even more on account of his spiritual vacuum that wants, believes in and hopes for nothing. This nihilism dehumanizes the beggar since it is a philosophical attitude, but as far as society is concerned, the result is pure anarchy. Espronceda appears to demand nothing less than a renewal of social values so that, without having to break any laws, man can live as a completely free individual integrated in the social milieu. Yet, lack of individual adherence to social authority, as the poet aspires, ultimately makes no sense; a limitless amount of personal liberty precludes the existence of a social body wherein every one of its members enjoys an equal amount of autonomy. The pessimism that weighs on the poet is patently evident in this satire against society carried out by an avenger whose post normally is the gutter but who, thanks to a total skepticism, lords over everyone. Espronceda approves the actions of one who, laughing at the established values, profits from them because he believes that society is constituted unfairly. The vision of man against the world, a leitmotiv in the «Canciones,» takes on a more mordant tone in «El mendigo» than in all the rest.

III. The Executioner and the Condemned Man

There can be no doubt as to Espronceda's humanism either in his life or in his writings. Ample testimony exists as to his charitable habits with the poor and no one can deny the selflessness with which he threw himself into the fray side by side with the liberal idealists seeking to topple oppressing regimes.[4] The commiseration with which the executioner and the criminal are viewed alludes directly to a censuring of the kind of society that engenders such deplorable injustices. The hangman, sufferer of the worst affrontery of all, had remained a forgotten and ominous figure in Spanish literature until Espronceda's poem. It is the poet himself who, assuming the identity of the executioner, takes on a subjective perspective in order to communicate from within the misery that outwardly has always been confused with heartless cruelty. Espronceda's verse bestows human warmth upon this traditionally abhorrent personnage and goes so far as to inspire tenderness in the reader's heart when, in a familial setting, the hangman's wife and son recognize the terrible legacy with which the latter is to be burdened.

The executioner, ironically, seems to be the victim rather than the instrument of death. Society empties its hatred and its desires for retribution onto him, forcing the wretch to carry out the most inhuman of punishments without regard for his own human conditions. The executioner is designated here as an instrument of social evil whose sentiments are dismissed, who is subsequently despised for his appointed profession and who ultimately faces nothing but ostracism and opprobrium. With the lines «En mí vive historia del mundo» and «Yo aún existo,/ fiel recuerdo de edades pasadas,» Espronceda suggests an unending trait through history—man's inhumanity to man. This indelible flaw that, by nature, drives man to transgress against his brother also has divine ascendancy which endows him with the capacity for evil. The poet does not hide the *imago Dei* condition by which man has always been known, thus showing skepticism of a just and merciful God capable of saving man from himself and the world, both equally imperfect. «El verdugo» turns out to be a conceitful metaphor symbolizing the seed of evil endemic for centuries in every man who is capable, as an individual, of infamy against his brother and, as a social being, of making his fellowmen victims of his own perversity.

The poem «El reo de muerte»—the longest (145 lines) and darkest in tone of all the «Canciones» so far considered—, aside from recalling an inhospitable and heartless Madrid, dovetails with the European romantic current not only in its usage of an indigent figure but also in its symbology of the prison as man's constricting microcosm.[5] The image had appeared previously with some regularity in Spanish poetry, above all in the *Romancero*. In this turn, the alienation from society is total. The despair felt by a prisoner in contrast with the uncaring indifference of the jailers who have sentenced him to the solitude foreboding death for a crime not even alluded to, demonstrates the profound disorientation towards life that, as a Romantic, anguished Espronceda. The crime, if one was committed, is not viewed as a motive for remorse, nor is the inevitable execution. The omnipresence of an ill fate hangs so heavily over the head of the prisoner that any effort to change its course seems doomed to failure. The only escape offered the condemned man is the dream where he can relive, however fleetingly, happier moments. But even this balm is withdrawn when in an absurd play of opposites the ominous silence of death row is broken by orgiastic cries outside the prison walls. The painful interruption serves to equate the external social disorder where nothing makes sense, with the nightmare and dream sequences that in hallucinatory fashion take place alternatively in the cell. Society's insensibility toward the prisoner wounds him to such a degree that, beside himself, the man curses his own existence, as well as life in general. Calderón's seventeenth-century dictum, voiced by the incarcerated prince Segismundo also while dreaming, that man's most terrible crime is to be born[6] takes on renewed meaning when one realizes the universal damnation Espronceda puts in the mouth of his character. He seems to have commited no crime other than that of having been born. Man's existence is a prison and the lot that awaits everyone is death. Consequently this would explain Espronceda's belief that the only possible attitude derivable from such a somber judgment is the damnation of human existence.[7] Blind fate has pushed the poet to denounce angrily life's lack of freedom of every sort—political, social, moral—concretely symbolized as a prison which debilitates him and ultimately ends his existence.

«El reo de muerte» is a poem of disillusionment, the final stop of the Esproncedian pessimism in its unequivocal negation of the established hierarchy of values. This is a radical pessimism whose sole object and subject is man. Espronceda remained totally unconcerned about the metaphysical ramifications that such a penchant for nihilism presupposes. What did preoccupy him, however, was the relationship between the individual and his social circumstance and, in a parallel manner, the correspondence between his sentimental self and the loved object—woman. In both instances it can be said that the poet considered man as locked into a perpetual struggle against society risking his freedom—i.e., life—whenever he heeds the institutional scale of values. Only a self-imposed alienation from the social body, either through the inversion of the above-mentioned scale of values on one's behalf as «El mendigo» points, or by removing oneself from the body politic as happens in «Canción del pirata,» can man save himself from amalgamation and the persecution of those who would take away his identity and his freedoms.

A rejection of the social order presupposes a search for a new mode of existence. Espronceda's answer was the kind of life where the individual affirms all of his liberties fully and at the expense of his fellowmen. However, as pointed out earlier, this alternative—far from being desirable or viable on account of its fundamentally contradictory nature—serves instead to uncover the anguish of a poet conscious of the crisis of his age and very personally affected by it. Sentiment and egocentrism rule supreme in Espronceda over reason and established social hierarchy.

IV. Three Socio-Political Compositions

«El canto del cosaco,» «El dos de mayo» and «A la traslación de las cenizas de Napoleón» are several steps removed from the four «Canciones» in terms of both structure and poetical perspective, yet their social and political implications justify their classification as *poésies engagées* much like those protagonized by the pirate, the beggar, the executioner and the condemned man.

«El canto del cosaco» never should have been included in the «Canciones» cycle by the critics for several reasons. In spite of the title, its protagonist is not one individual but a large band of barbarians. Absolute individual liberty of any sort does not enter into the picture. Its verse structure of paired hendecasyllabic *cuartetas* follows a traditional format. Finally, as was pointed out above, its date of composition came some four years later than the others, having first appeared on December 15, 1838 in Barcelona's *El Guardia Nacional*. And yet «El canto del cosaco,» in spite of everything, probably appeals to the same audience that relished the bold figures of the earlier outcasts. Hostility to the social status quo remains the life blood of this poetry. The anarchistic sentiment in «El canto del cosaco» is expressed in terms of one people—a horde of cossack barbarians that Espronceda confused with Atilla's Huns, judging by the epigraph attributed to the latter[8]—bent on plundering the whole of Western Europe. That the poet allied himself with the invaders has little to do with the now-familiar romantic notions (egocentrism, sentimentality, liberty); instead, the choice of sides has much to do with the punishment of a decadent society that succumbed to a world ruled by pleasure and gold. The invading cossacks—the pounding of their horses' hooves echoed in the alternating assonance of even-numbered verses with odd ones rhyming consonantally—function as a whip[9] to shake Europe out of its materialism. The continent is viewed as a host of nations forgetful of any higher ideal, which eventually will mean its internal destruction as a civilization, an ethical consideration that kept Espronceda from advocating its annihilation; the Cossacks have nothing to offer in substitution. Strength, fearlessness and a thirst for glory do not suffice and are used only as a measure of contrast to bring out the weak, cowardly and mercenary attitudes that governed Europe's social values. That a romantic poet confronted socio-economic matters may seem strange enough, but that he did so in a poem is something few could achieve with the degree of success Espronceda has.

Of similarly intemperate and exalted tone is the poem «El dos de mayo» in which Espronceda praised the courage of the populace in the war of Independence against Napoleon fought in the years 1808 to 1814. The composition appeared on the thirty-second anniversary of the resistance in the Madrid journal *El Labriego*, occupying its entire front page and framed in black to resemble an obituary. Lest anyone miss the point, its political intention was thus established. As he had done before in «A la patria,» Espronceda turned to a glorious historical moment—May 2, 1808—and then back to a «dismal present,»[10] a sweeping thirty-year survey written in thirty-seven hendecasyllabic *serventesios*. Beginning with his earliest recollections as a child told by his parents, the poet on the one hand extols the common citizens who, though ill-armed, fought to the death against the machine-like troops of the self-proclaimed Emperor, conqueror of Europe, so vividly depicted in one of Goya's most memorable canvasses. But, then, as in the poet's own time, Spain was betrayed by those—mostly in the upper classes—who sought safety in arrangements compromising to Spain's honor. These were above all Carlos IV's prime minister, Manuel Godoy, who was the adulterous Queen's favorite, his own son and heir Fernando VII, and all of those who from then until the present looked upon the French not as the enemy but as a means to resolve national conflicts no matter how subservient to a foreign power the solutions might be. Espronceda's ire brands them as traitors, cowards and sycophants, a denigrating characterization that not even France's Louis Phillippe escapes when he is labelled «rey mercader.»

«El dos de mayo» is a paean on behalf of the popular cause. On the day it was published it served as an eloquent endorsement of a popular constitution then under consideration.[11] But on a more universal plane, the poem extols the bravery of a people sometimes despised by others for whom patriotism meant nothing if comfort and position did not exist alongside it. And above all these verses point to May 2nd, 1808 as a victory for those willing to lose their lives when the nation's independence was at stake despite those who not only ran away from the fight but actually sought a pact with the enemy. The last quartet pleads that the noble blood of the populace shall not have been spilled in vain.

Though shorter than either «El canto del cosaco» or «El dos de mayo,» « A la traslación de las cenizas de Napoleón» shares with them not only several nearly identical lines but also continues a bitter denunciation of the Continent's turning away from civilized higher ideals. This poem's other title as it appears in some editions, «A la degradación de Europa,» rightly gauges its creator's «moral indignation.»[12] The stridency and despair of its tone outdoes the other two compositions in this regard. Here, the vision of Europe contemplated as a «fetid cadaver» on a «rotten heart» resembles, at one moment, a post mortem and, the next, apocalypse. In the former instance the poet's voice turns disconsolate as his eyes sweep over a panorama of decadence and spiritual contamination. Mammon has usurped all loftier ideals because everything is measured in terms of profit: nations have turned into markets, heroes and poets have been displaced by traders. In the last three strophes the poet, alone among desolate cold ashes, becomes a prophet reborn to dispel the apocalypse, cursing the merchants and the profiteers, and summoning others under the spell of gold to return to a more humanistic existence that only true ideals can provide. «Un cádaver no más es vuestra gloria» proclaims the last verse of the poem, chastising those who, overcome by greed and the profit motive, have accomplished nothing short of turning a civilization into ashes. The title «A la traslación de las cenizas de Napoleón» is, thus, also the poem's greatest metaphor. Napoleon, who by conquering Europe, destroyed it as a fecund civilization and ultimately himself, now serves, upon the return of his ashes to France, as an admonishment of what lay in store for Europeans, if indeed that day was not already upon them.

With the four «Canciones» and these last three poems, it can be said that Espronceda's mature verse has come into its own. These poems represent the rebellious or reformist Romanticism as its best. No longer does Espronceda conceive poetry taken as a rhetorical game,[13] it has now become a vehicle for ideals. The pirate, the beggar, the executioner and the condemned man may be romantic figures for their boldness, their arrogance or their individualism, but they also fulfill a very clear ethical purpose—however mistated or exaggerated—, which is to emphasize man's inalienable right to political, social, economic and moral liberty. «El canto del cosaco,» «El dos de mayo,» and «A la traslación de las cenizas de Naopleon,» while employing some of the least poetic or romantic themes such as crematistic concerns in detriment of idealistic ones, attest to Espronceda's growing social as well as humanistic ideology, a philosophy that he did not consider antithetical to the romantic credo. After all, he continued to exhibit in these compositions Romanticism's major preoccupation—a dissatisfaction with reality when compared to its more desireable and perhaps possible resemblance to an ideal.

An equally evolutionary linguistic and structural format, exhibiting a more simplified language devoid of flourishes, almost stark in its dearth of rhetorical figures, and in the usage of metrics never so fully and unusually exploited previously, make this cluster of poems stand out not only among Espronceda's poems but also among those of all Spanish Romantics.

NOTES

1. Alex Preminger et. al., eds. *Princeton Encyclopedia of Poetry and Poetics* (Princeton, 1972), p. 469.

2. Morse Peckham, «Toward a Theory of Romanticism,» *PMLA*, 66 (March 1961), 1-8.

3. *Poesías líricas y fragmentos épicos,* Marrast, ed., p. 37.

4. Walter T. Pattison, «On Espronceda's Personality,» *PMLA*, 61 (2946), 1141.

5. Donald L. Shaw, «Towards the Understanding of Spanish Romanticism,» *Modern Language Review* 58 (April 1963), 194.

6. Segismundo: «pues el delito mayor / del hombre es haber nacido.» *La vida es sueño* (I, 2), Martín de Riquer, ed. (Barcelona, 1961), p. 61.

7. Donald L. Shaw, *op. cit.,* p. 194.

8. *Poesías líricas y fragmentos épicos,* Marrast ed., p. 254.

9. Joaquín Casalduero, *Espronceda* (Madrid, 1967), p. 157.

10. Gabriel H. Lovett, «The War of Independence (1808-1814) in 19th Century Spanish Poetry.» *Revista de Estudios Hispánicos* 10 (May 1976), 227.

11. Enrique Piñeyro, «Espronceda,» 5 (1930), p. 420. In this article the author

points out that, aside from *El Diablo Mundo,* «Al dos de mayo» was the only other poem not included in the first edition (May 1840) of Espronceda's *Poesías.*

12. Casalduero, *op. cit.,* p. 118.

13. *Poesías líricas y fragmentos épicos,* Marrast ed., p. 38.

CHAPTER FIVE

Sentimental and Meditative Poetry

In the totality of his verse production, one of its constants, the sentimental, expresses Espronceda's growing pessimism as years go by and his bitterness resulting from love's disillusionment. From the semihopeful, sweet and nostalgic love song in the early sonnet «Fresca, lozana, pura y olorosa,» his muse turns gradually to resentful songs of indifference toward life and damnation of the loved one or erotic object, as in «A Jarifa en una orgía,» where Espronceda's own suffering is beyond doubt. This trajectory suggests an increasing realization of the abyss separating what he as a poet is able to fantasize and what he as a man has within reach.

Because Romanticism is a system of contradictions amounting to an aesthetics of sentiments,[1] the muse of romantic poetry is sentimental exaltation. We owe to Teresa Mancha, the *femme fatale* of Espronceda's love life, the inspiration for one of the most valued groups of his verses, the emotional or love lyric. The subject corresponding to this lyric will always be a woman, whom the poet identifies and confuses with love itself.[2]

I. Love and Roses in Their Prime

The sonnet, preferred lyric form of Spanish Renaissance and Baroque literatures, is rarely used by this country's Romantics who shied away from its rigid structure. Its fixed form does not allow a free-flowing rhythm, demanding instead a sober and restrained language. Bécquer wrote only two[3] and not very successfully, while Espronceda produced nine.[4] Written before he was twenty (1826-27),[5] and known alternately by its first verse «Fresca, lozana, pura y olorosa» or by the title «Rosas y esperanzas,» the composition constitutes Espronceda's first great love poem.

This sonnet (ABBA ABBA CDE CDE) remains relatively faithful to classical canons, not only on account of its structure but also because of its central metaphor on the theme «rosa-ilusión de amor.» All of the great Spanish Renaissance and Golden Age sonneteers had treated the *tempus fugit topos* earlier: Garcilaso with his Sonnet XXIII, «En tanto que de rosa y azucena»; Quevedo's Sonnet «A Flora»; Góngora's Sonnets XCIV («Vana rosa»), XCV («A la rosa y su brevedad») and his famous «Mientras por competir con tu cabello»; turning to another literature, Shakespeare's «Venus and Adonis» contains perhaps the best known lines of this theme in English: «Fair flowers that are not gather'd in their prime/ Rot and consume themselves in little time.» But none of these compositions come so close to Espronceda's handling of the subject as Pierre Ronsard's sonnet from the *Amours I* (1555) collection, subsequently retouched and included in his *Amours II* (1578-87). The similarity between the Frenchman's and the Spaniard's first quatrains are nothing short of amazing.

> Douce, belle, amoureuse, et bien-fleurante Rose,
> Que tu es a bon droit aux amours consacrée!
> Ta delicate odeur hommes et Dieux recrée,
> Et bref, Rose, tu es belle sur toute chose. (v. 1-4)[6]

* * *

> Fresca, lozana, pura y olorosa,
> gala y adorno del pensil florido,
> gallarda puesta sobre el ramo erguido,
> fragancia esparce la naciente rosa. (v. 1-4)

Nevertheless, unhindered by all of its antecedents, Espronceda's sonnet is infused with unusual freeness, with a note of subtle sensuality ideally suited to a young love. The poem contains two united or connected thoughts: the delight derived from the rose's beauty, and sorrow at its ephemeral existence, both present in the quatrains. The parallel course followed by love, hope and then the pain of love's loss, is insinuated in the tercets. This sonnet is distinguished from the poet's secondary poems by virtue of its singular lyrical lexicon, foreshadowing the simplicity and spontaneity of expression characteristic of Espronceda's later verse. Its fundamentally romantic character can be appreciated in the play of opposites which functions in terms of the metaphor of the rose and poet's love (freshness-flaccidity, hope-despair) concordant with the bimembrated structure already noted above.

As the initial milestone of the autor's sentimental itinerary, this sonnet enunciates the belief that love carries a fateful burden of sadness, even if temporarily alleviated by illusion. As time passes, this initial dose of illusion will diminish progressively while the implied bitterness turns into total despair.

II. Ascending Despair

Of a more tranquil nature because of its quietly discursive tone so infrequent in Espronceda, «A una estrella» pursues serenely for one hundred and twenty verses of a tripartite arrangement the poet's path of love from incipient happiness:

> ¡Ay, lucero! yo te ví
> resplandecer en mi frente,
> cuando palpitar sentí
> mi corazón dulcemente
> con amante frenesí. (v. 29-33)

through the sadness and grief as a result of the loss of the beloved:

> Mas ¡ay! que luego el bien y la alegría
> en llanto y desventura se trocó. (v. 21-22)'

to end in a glacial apathy as seen in the last strophe:

> Yo indiferente sigo mi camino
> a merced de los vientos y la mar,
> y entregado en los brazos del destino,
> ni me importa salvarme o zozobrar. (v. 116-120)

When Espronceda recited this poem for the first time on July 5, 1838, at a meeting of the literary Liceo of Madrid, his first separation from Teresa had already taken place. This loss which touched the poet so deeply is a much more likely source of inspiration than either José Bermúdez de Castro's «A una estrella misteriosa» or Lord Byron's «Sun of the Sleepless,» as some critics have asserted. '

In romantic poetry, love is typically either impossible or ephemeral. In «A una estrella» the second is true. The poem constitutes a dialectical lament about the joy and sorrows shared between the poet and a star. The latter comes to represent the former's hopes, refulgent when the lover feels joyful and dark when he senses himself abandoned, in an obvious pathetic fallacy. «Stellar light—lover's happiness» then is the central metaphor of the poem, uniting both subjects. The anthropomorphic star projects the poet's nostalgia and grief, so that the «timidity,» «sadness,» «youth» and «melancholy» attributed to it are but a reflection of his mood. The poet, withdrawn and hermetic, seeks the company of the star as a silent consolation following his amorous disillusionment. The star, visualized as faithful, elevates love to an idealized plane with the perpetuity and radiance of its light. On the other hand, human love suffers fatally the same mortality as those who experience it, rarely achieving the desired perfection. Consequently, incapable of reconciling his dream of love with the reality of man's destiny, the poet involuntarily retreats from life.

In the first two poems Espronceda avoided all sentimental stridency. In «Fresca, lozana, pura y olorosa,» with traces of youthful optimism, he harbors the possible hope that a love may exist capable of uplifting man even if the joy derived lasts ever so briefly. The sustained but controlled tone of «A una estrella» manifests the growth of the pessimistic concept of love which had begun to grip the poet. The certainty of an irrevocable despair ultimately leading to a *tedium vitae* was the new attitude from which Espronceda thenceforth would not stray.

III. Love Madness

The composed tones of amorous sentiment characterizing the two foregoing poems disappear, to be replaced by the agitation and violence animating «A Jarifa en una orgía.» The most bitter of all poems from Espronceda's pen, as well as his best-known after «Canción del pirata,» it allows no ray of hope to dispel the gloom over its one hundred and sixteen verses. In «Jarifa» the poet feels cheated by deficient reality, convinced that it does not respond to his aspirations. Having tried time and again to satisfy his desires he has found nothing but deception. Short of death—«Huya la vida/ paz me traiga el ataúd»—the romantic can expect little else which will not deceive him in the world. Essaying other means of grasping what he longs for, the poet becomes much like the drug addict who comes to loathe his dependency on an intoxicating dosage:

> Y aturdan mi revuelta fantasía
> los brindis y el estruendo del festín
> y huya la noche y me sorprenda el día
> en un letargo estúpido y sin fin. (v. 105-108)

The poet finds himself a prisoner, against his will, of the passions of an imperfect and impure love that ultimately jades his life. Woman, a demonical figure and source of a love that is damned, does not fit the poet's dream as he despairs for having once conceived a pure love. The spiritual passion exists solely in his heart. Once manifested or externalized it becomes hopelessly stained.

And so the contemplated joy turns to grief:

> Y encontré mi ilusión desvanecida,
> y eterno e insaciable mi deseo.
> Palpé la realidad y odié la vida:
> sólo en la paz de los sepulcros creo. (v. 72-76)

The beloved degenerates into a whore:

> Mujeres vi de virginal limpieza
> entre albas nubes de celeste lumbre;
> yo las toqué, y en humo su pureza
> trocarse vi, y en lodo y podredumbre. (v. 69-72)

The flower becomes a thorn and all that man cherishes he receives in a horrid and distorted image. Charged with a cynicism that cannot be far removed from the poet's troubled psyche, the poem recalls the somber tone of Hogarth's woodcuts in *The Rake's Progress.*[9]

During the search for a love concordant with his desires, Espronceda falls into the morass of eroticism and suffocating sensuality. Happiness lies beyond the realm of palpable reality. Pleasure and hope are, alas, but chimeras that man cannot avoid despite the grief and disenchantment which never fail to follow. Thus, the poet, forced to renounce the dreams of his internal world, allows himself to be seduced by a sensual orgy—alcohol, stupefying drugs, or any deadening of the senses—that will bring on a blissful state of ataraxia,

> ni el placer ni la tristura
> vuelvan mi pecho a turbar. (v. 95-96)

as he seeks to assuage the bitterness of disillusionment. In this fashion
Espronceda avoids the «peace that awaits in the sepulchre,» a decision
amounting to a renunciation of all that which his inner turmoil dictates.
The poet withdraws from his defiant stance to seek the company of Jarifa,
a woman wounded by the same annihilating perception:

> Ven, Jarifa; tú has sufrido
> como yo; tú nunca lloras.
> Mas ¡ay, triste! que no ignoras
> Cuán amarga es nuestra aflicción.
> Una misma es nuestra pena,
> en vano el llanto contienes...
> Tú también, como yo, tienes
> desgarrado el corazón. (v. 109-116)

The arms of Jarifa,[10] a being equally burned by despair and suffering,
are in this poem the sought-after consolation to the poet's ennui.

IV. Teresa as the Tainted Beauty[11]

Espronceda's despair, so patent in the love-madness of «A Jarifa» and
renewed in the «Canto a Teresa»[12] is profoundly rooted in the perennial
dichotomy between vital reality and the reality conceived by the poet's imagination or sentiment. The inevitable result of this dilemma is the destruction of idealistic aspirations and the poet's consequent demoralization.
Espronceda hits a raw nerve when dealing with the theme of love, proof of
the abyss that separated his dream from everyday life.

The «Canto a Teresa» is the second part of a larger work, *El Diablo
Mundo,* a section which the poet himself admitted had very little to do with
the rest of the whole.[13] There is no reason to doubt Espronceda's sincerity
in his invitation for the reader to skip it when reading *El Diablo Mundo.*

The «Canto a Teresa» does not represent an attempt to resolve the
conflict between runaway idealism and impure reality, as was the case in
«A Jarifa en una orgía» where the question is first posed, but simply exposes that antagonism in terms of personal despair and vilifying cruelty
toward the loved one.[14] The «Canto» and, to a lesser degree perhaps, «A
Jarifa» were both motivated by the ill-fated outcome of the love between
the poet and Teresa. Both poems clearly stand as autobiographical. She,
whom Espronceda met as a teenager when he was barely twenty, was to re-

main as his sweet sorrow even after their separation and her death soon thereafter in the saddest and most dissolute misery as a degraded prostitute.

The poet, a resentful lover, struggled to rid himself of a grief attributable less to the death of Teresa than to his own prior loss of love for her, due to her fall from the pedestal where Espronceda had placed her.[15] His suffering, therefore, results not so much from the corporal death but rather from the demise of his love for Teresa when she ceased to exist as beloved because of her inescapable condition as a woman of flesh and blood. Her descent from Eve causes her to become the souless and pervese woman of the poem, a characterization that, in real life, probably did not fit Teresa in the least.

The first elegy written by Espronceda, «A la patria» grieved over Spain's decline into misery on account of the infamous reign of Fernando VII. The «Canto a Teresa» is Espronceda's last elegiac composition. If the former was far from being a full-blown romantic poem, the second is perhaps the least unorthodox among his most famous verses. Its *octava real* structure, as well as the use of the *ubi sunt?*, *carpe diem* and other Renaissance and Baroque topics, conforms perfectly to the traditional mold of the elegy, in and of itself a very venerable formal lyric composition originated by the Greeks and omnipresent in Spanish literature.[16] It will be remembered that among the Romantics, Zorrilla was catapulted to fame by his elegy «A la muerte de Larra,» read at the suicide's tomb. This funeral held on February 15, 1837 was attended by every major literary figure in Madrid except by Espronceda who was ill at the time.[17] In this type of composition, memory completely absorbs the attention of the poet, and Espronceda's remembrances during the forty-four *octavas reales* of the «Canto» are immediate and intimate. The theory of the poem's two different dates of composition is by now well-known and generally accepted.[18] The first writing corresponds to the eighteen inaugural strophes inspired by the separation of the two lovers and the second section motivated by the death of Teresa. This lapse, if we are to believe it existed, does not diminish the total impact; on the contrary, sentimental content increases with the interval, revealing the vastly different reactions of the poet to the two most painful jolts of his existence. In the first part Espronceda dwells upon the remembered happiness of a shared love; in the second, he laments the loss of this love and rails against the beloved. The twenty-fifth strophe synthesizes this interpretation thus:

> ....
> Tú fuiste un tiempo cristalino río,
> manantial de purísima limpieza;

> después torrente de color sombrío,
> ....
> y estanque, en fin, de aguas corrompidas,
> entre fétido fango detenidas. (v. 1694-1699)

The last three lines best characterize the mood of the final portion while the first two could very well serve to illustrate the opening segment of the «Canto.»

Whereas in the first section the lover's longings for a pure and eternal love appear, in the final portion the poet's disillusionment and vituperation of the loved one for not possessing at once the qualities of Aphrodite and Madonna are most memorable. Such is the form taken by the constant struggle between Espronceda's inner self and outer reality. The poet's egotism cannot be overstated. Espronceda weeps more at the impossiblity of fulfilling his own desires than for the death of Teresa—dead for him when she is no longer able to be the idolized woman. He damns her yet is unable to forget her; his heart is wounded but not free of her. He says as much in the first strophe, thus continuing the love-hate antilogy:

> ¿Por qué volvéis a la memoria mía,
> tristes recuerdos del placer perdido,
> a aumentar la ansiedad y la agonía
> de este desierto corazón herido?
> ....(v. 1500-1508)

Espronceda intends thereby to be as cruel with her as he avers she was with him in revealing herself as only human. In his passionate, blind egocentrism—v. 1628: «es el amor que al mismo amor adora»—the poet subjugates every concept of woman and love to one aspect which allows no modification: the candid and beautiful woman, a celestial creature of pure fantasy, too perfect to be real. Naturally, the imagined beauty would turn to dust when the poet discovered the Edenic caste—poisoned by the apple and the serpent—of his beloved. The sin attributed to her, alluded to in the antipenultimate strophe—v. 1829: «¡Espantosa expiación de tu pecado!»—is, then, not only Eve's own, but the defraudation of the poet: Teresa turned out to be neither god-like nor virginal.

Espronceda tried in many ways to reduce human existence exclusively to an amorous dimension, since in the mind of many Romantics love can redeem man. Zorrilla's Don Juan, rescued from the eternal flames by his sincere love for Doña Inés, is a case in point and one to be contrasted with the manner in which Tirso disposed of his Don Juan—casting him into Hell by the hand of the man he had injured most, Doña Inés' father, the Comendador. But Espronceda always found exiguous for his thirst the love within his grasp. He was not satisfied, because he could never satiate his wants with what was for him mediocre reality. Love having failed him as a means whereby to rescue his existence from banality, Espronceda abandoned himself to follow cynically and indifferently the course of the world around him. This explains why not only the «Canto a Teresa» but other poems including «A una estrella» and «A Jarifa» end on notes of wounded indifference. For the poet, powerless against the world, there remains only the sleep of the sepulchre or drifting with the current like other mortals since all struggle with fate is futile. The climax of such an attitude is the empty defiance of the last verse, «Que haya un cadáver más, ¡qué importa al mundo!», whose pained sarcasm is all too obvious.

In his love lyrics Espronceda was unable to reconcile his views of his world. Nor did he know how to orient his own life in order to harmonize his inner world—which nurtured his poetry—with external reality, and so it follows that continuity and intermittence can be jointly observed in his life as well as in his work. He remained unaware of how to adapt himself to the reality in which he was forced to dwell. The resultant shock of the encounter between the two worlds produced an enduring sorrow, making him pessimistic and darkening his verse. His disenchantment with life is thus not surprising. The dissatisfaction of a romantic spirit such as Espronceda's stems from that stance which arbitrarily pretended to reduce all meaning to an extremely subjective and personal vantage point, producing a capricious tedium, a universal skepticism and ultimate damnation of the woman beloved.

NOTES

1. Julián Marías, *Historia de la filosofía* (Madrid, 1967), p. 321.
2. Esteban Pujals, *Espronceda y Lord Byron* (Madrid, 1972), p. 36.
3. Gustavo Adolfo Bécquer's two sonnets, written in his youth, were: «Al Céfiro» and «Homero cante a quien su lira Clío.»
4. Espronceda's sonnets, in chronological order, are: «La noche,» «A Eva,» «Bajas de la cascada, undosa fuente,» «Fresca, lozana, pura y olorosa,» «A la muerte de Torrijos y sus compañeros,» «A un ruiseñor,» «A una mariposa,» «A xxx dedicándolo estas poesías,» «A Guardia.»
5. *Poesías líricas y fragmentos épicos,* Marrast ed., pp. 119-21.

6. For further reference see K.R.W. Jones, *Pierre de Ronsard* (Boston, 1970), pp. 58-60 and p. 150.

7. Compare these with verses 12-13 of «Fresca, lozana, pura y olorosa.»

8. See especially Philip H. Churchman, «Byron and Espronceda,» *Revue Hispanique*, 20 (1909), 149-50; Pujals, *op. cit.*, pp. 443-45; Daniel G. Samuels, «Fuentes de 'A una estrella' de Espronceda,» *Horizontes* (July 1941), 36-41 and also his «Some Spanish Romantic Debts of José de Espronceda,» *Hispanic Review*, 16 (1948), 157-58.

9. I am grateful to Professor Bruce W. Wardropper of Duke University for suggesting this connection to me some years ago.

10. Jarifa's true identity has been forever in dispute. It isn't likely it was Teresa, dead for almost two years (18 September 1839). Better candidates were Carmen Soler, the woman Espronceda was seeing at the time, or else Carmen Ossorio to whom the poet dedicated his *Poesías* volume in 1840. So opines R. Marrast in his edition of the *Poesías líricas y fragmentos épicos,* note 163, p. 259. Churchman (*op. cit.,* pp. 155-56) and Pujals (*op. cit.,* pp. 445-47) argue on opposite sides of the question as to whether Byron, in this case «To Inez» from the *Childe Harold*, or Shakespearse's Sonnet LXVI was the real inspiration for «A Jarifa.»

11. See Mario Praz, *The Romantic Agony*, 2nd edition (London and New York, 1970), especially the chapter entitled «The Beauty of the Medusa,» pp. 25-52, for a discussion of the romantic heroines.

12. Unamuno in his most celebrated comment on Espronceda denied the sincerity and depth of the poet's thought remarking that: «His *[*Espronceda's*]* famous despair, a la Byron, was more rhetorical and literary than anything. Espronceda could have had no doubt about certain things because he never thought seriously about them.» *Mi religión y otros ensayos. Obras completas IV* (Madrid, 1958), p. 488.

13. Espronceda appended a footnote to the title saying: «This *canto* is an unburdening of my heart, skip it over without scruples whoever does not wish to read it because it isn't connected in any way to the Poem.»

14. Bruce W. Wardropper, «Espronceda's *Canto a Teresa* and the Spanish Elegiac Tradition,» *Bulletin of Hispanic Studies,* 40 (1963), 89.

15. *Ibid., p. 89ff.*

16. Wardropper, *op. cit.,* p. 90. For further discussion on the elegy see Alex Preminger, et. al., eds., *Princeton Encyclopedia of Poetry and Poetics* (Princeton, 1972), pp. 215-217.

17. Jean-Louis Picoche, *Un romántico español: Enrique Gil y Carrasco* (Madrid, 1978), pp. 34-35.

18. There are differing opinions on the subject. Casalduero and Marrast remain silent, Pujals fixes the cut on the twenty-fifth stanza, Cascales agrees to the two-part theory but does not say which stanza divides the poem. I feel that the eighteenth

stanza marks the dividing line because of the content (pleasant memories of the love enjoyed), tone (tempered) and attitude (melancholy) that subsequently change noticeably, becoming charged with bitterness, egocentrism and vituperation.

CHAPTER SIX

The Longest Poems: The Best and The Impossible

Of the two longest verse works written by Espronceda, one turned out to be a remarkable masterpiece and the other an admirable failure. The former, *El Estudiante de Salamanca,* is widely considered to be among the most perfect examples of romantic dramatic poems: complete unto itself, animated by well-developed characters, and blessed with a dizzying unfolding of events. The latter, *El Diablo Mundo,* remains merely an attempt to chronicle man's progress in the world from the time of the creation to the modern age—clearly an effort superior to the strength of the poet who died perhaps years before he could have hoped to complete it. In the case of *El Estudiante de Salamanca,* Espronceda, without having chosen a remotely ambitious theme, succeeded beyond measure in the creation of a new version of the traditional irreverent and womanizing rogue that is Don Juan. In the case of *El Diablo Mundo,* while deliberately attempting to conquer a grand theme—the history of mankind, he failed magnificently since it is doubtful, judging by the seven cantos left behind, whether a completed work would have meant any more than the scarcely begun remnants.

I. History, Plot and Sources of *El Estudiante de Salamanca*

Espronceda began working on *El Estudiante de Salamanca* early in 1836 and, although he did not finish the 1,704 verse poem until 1840 when it was published alongside his other poetry in the volume *Poesías,* a first partial version appeared in the magazine *El Español*, on March 7, 1836. The following year the complete first part (v. 1-179) was published in Madrid's *Museo Artístico y Literario* in the June 22 issue. That the writing of this work was constant throughout the four years from 1836 to 1840 can be garnered by further fragmentary issuings of *El Estudiante de Salamanca* surfacing in various Spanish newspapers and magazines during this time, as well as by readings that the poet gave of his work in progress such as the one recorded in Granada on June 22, 1837.[1]

This long poem, subtitled «Cuento,» has a most traditional plot built around the Don Juan character conceived by the Mercedarian friar Tirso de Molina (*né* Gabriel Téllez) and first seen in his play *El burlador de Sevilla y convidado de piedra*. In Espronceda's work Don Félix de Montemar, a Salamanca University student, notorious lover, swordsman and gambler, seduces Doña Elvira de Pastrana who, once forgotten by him, goes insane and withers away from lost love. Her brother, Don Diego de Pastrana, seeking to avenge Elvira's dishonor and death, perishes at the hands of Don Félix. The latter, also mortally wounded in the duel, dies, having undergone a hallucinating agony on his way to Hell (where his tomb resembles a nuptial bed) and having witnessed his own funeral accompanied by Elvira's skeletal ghost. Most of the themes, some of the characters and a few of the situations are already quite familiar and indeed Espronceda's originality in *El Estudiante de Salamanca* does not reside in these ingredients but rather in the spirit of the tale, its concept of the world and in its shattering finale.

Among the most striking themes seen here are first of all the vision of one's own funeral. This leitmotiv had been dealt with rather frequently by Golden Age playwrights such as Vélez de Guevara in his *El niño diablo*, Lope de Vega's *El vaso de elección, San Pablo* and Calderón de la Barca's *El purgatorio de San Patricio*. Nearer to Espronceda's time one finds in the nineteenth century two very popular ballads based on the wayward life of Lisardo, a student from Córdoba, whose infamous notoriety had already been documented by Cristóbal Lozano in his *Soledades de la vida y desengaños del mundo* in the seventeenth century and one hundred years earlier by Antonio de Torquemada in his *Jardín de flores curiosas*. José García de Villalta, a close friend of Espronceda and co-editor of his first volume of *Poesías,* similarly included a passage in his own novel *El golpe en vago* where the main character is a witness to his own funeral.[2] Since García de Villalta's book antedates Espronceda's completion of *El Estudiante de Salamanca* by five years there can be no question as to the latter's knowledge of it. More problematic is the case of Zorrilla's verse legend *El capitán Montoya,* where a similar incident occurs, since this poem was published after Espronceda's own but its author claimed to have read it early in 1839 at Madrid's Liceo, a literary club often frequented by Espronceda. Who plagiarized whom?

The motiv of the woman skeleton can be found in Mira de Amescua's

El esclavo del demonio and especially in Gonzalo Céspedes y Meneses' story *La constante Cordobesa* from his collection titled *Historias peregrinas y ejemplares*. Here the protagonists' names are Elvira and Don Diego, the former corresponding to Espronceda's heroine and the second one, though belonging to the hero in Céspedes story, was used by Espronceda to designate Elvira's brother.

Many other themes such as the heroine's insanity on account of love, the horrifying *danse macabre* and the theme of honor are easily traceable to numerous periods, genres and authors not only in Spanish but in world literature, and it would be foolhardy to attempt any commentary here in view of their vastness.[3] On the other hand, though perhaps no less imposing in terms of its manifold and extensive use, the likeliest sources for the character of Don Félix cannot go unmentioned at this point.

Foremost is the above-mentioned Don Juan of Tirso de Molina after whom hundreds of rogues are patterned in almost every nation's literature. But chances are that Espronceda had two other characters in mind when gestating his own. One was the Córdoba-born student, Lisardo, whose picaresque life in the University City of Salamanca had been recounted in books and ballads for nearly three hundred years. The second one was Don Miguel de Mañara, a legendary figure who lived in Seville in the mid-1600's and whose fabled and dissolute life was chronicled in both fiction by Prosper Mérimée in his *Les Âmes du purgatorie* and in biography by the Jesuit Juan de Cárdenas in *Breve relación de la muerte, vida y virtudes de D. Miguel de Mañara* and later by José Gutiérrez de la Vega, a contemporary of Espronceda. At least in the first of the last two accounts, the name of the street where Mañara died, *Calle del Ataúd,* is mentioned, a name that Espronceda used in his poem. Futhermore there can be no doubt as to Mañara's parentage, real or imagined, since in the fragment prepublished (June 22, 1937) in the *Museo Artístico y Literario* magazine, verse number 100 which reads «Segundo don Juan Tenorio,» referring to Don Félix, at that time read «Nuevo don Juan *[sic]* de Marana *[sic].*»

II. The Romantic Figure of a Satanic Titan

Don Félix, true enough, possesses a great many of the characteristics that are most memorable about his predecessors and which have given all of the known Don Juans such extraordinary popularity and longevity. Aside from his undeniable stature as the rich scion of a noble family, he is a handsome libertine—arrogant, bold and cynical. But from here the qualities he shares with the stereotype diminish as the core of his soul is reached. Like his confreres, Don Félix feels indifferent toward death and lives only for the present—v. 934: «Para mí no hay nunca mañana ni ayer»—embodying perfectly the ancient *topos* and the *carpe diem* that confers on all of these romantic male figures an air of immortality, so that even when they are cut down, they die at the prime of their life and are remembered as vigorous young men untouched by the ravages of time. In keeping with their defiance of and indifference to death Don Félix, as a romantic hero, causes the death of women through his irresistible charm and that of other men through his virtuosity with the sword, usually without meaning to or even mattering to him. For example in *El Estudiante de Salamanca,* Don Félix ignores Doña Elvira's demise, which resulted from his spurning of her, until he is made aware of it by her brother Don Diego in the Parte Tercera (v. 605-616).

At this point Don Félix no longer has much in common with the archetypal Don Juan figure. Whereas the prototypical Don Juan believes in God, having an almost excessive faith in his mercy—which accounts for the rogue's damnation in Tirso's case thinking that there will always be plenty of time to repent—even if he breaks divine as well as mens' laws, Don Félix stands up to God and challenges His authority. This supreme rebelliousness sets Don Félix apart from any other romantic figure. «El personaje de Espronceda es la encarnación del Anticristo a lo romántico»⁴ because his boundless energy, so characteristic of the other Don Juans, here is channeled into a sacrilegious defiance of the Almighty in a satanic fashion:

> Con Dios le iguala, y con osado vuelo
> se alza a su trono y le provoca a duelo.
> Segundo Lucifer que se levanta... (v. 1251-1253)

That Don Félix does not submit to God even in death is sufficient cause even for Espronceda, the unwavering paladin of individual freedom, as we saw in the «Canciones» cycle, to have him damned for all eternity—unless, of course, one is to think that burning in Hell is preferable to yielding one's innermost convictions even if the one who demands that submission is the Almighty himself.

As a God is how Doña Elvira looks upon Don Félix: (v. 178-179) «embriagada /Elvira/ del dios que la enamora,/ dulce le mira, extática le adora.» In other words a second Satan who exacts adoration from those under his spell, and who, like the Prince of Darkness, cannot be trusted for he brings death, not joy. Elvira is a victim of Don Félix' deceit; not loving Elvira, he merely seduces her and, having succeeded, abandons her in his role as a conqueror of women. Subsequently, she succumbs to her own remorse for having fallen so willingly to his advances. In her virtuousness Elvira considers her death, coming while still so young and immediately after Don Félix' departure, as an expiation for her passion for Montemar. It is this ingenuous belief in atonement that accounts for virginal whiteness—with which numerous times her wandering soul is characterized as it leads Montemar on his chase to the house of death—as well as the reward that ultimately she gains when after her death she becomes Don Félix' bride and the instrument of his death as he had been of hers. Her virtue triumphs in the end in a macabre personification of a mythical Death-Beloved.

Like most romantic heroines Elvira exists in a contrapuntal fashion to the hero: she is pure, faithful and loving while he is profane, promiscuous and depraved. Still, Elvira, though she embodies an innocence so complete that Don Félix easily succeeds in deflowering her (v. 263-272, 355), posesses another dimension that makes her more credible—her passionateness. This duality of passion and purity, already pointed out by Casalduero,[5] creates a more significant and empathetic role for Elvira. She does not wish to merely languish in love for Don Félix, she wants him passionately and is hurt when he no longer has any interest in her.

III. Narrative and Sequential Structure

El Estudiante de Salamanca, through written in the late 1830s, in its chronologically fragmented order of events could be considered a product of the 20th century where time sequence is frequently disrupted by an author for purposes of either simulating the chaos that the events bring about or else to lend importance to certain actions that normally would be overshadowed by others intrinsically more striking. So it happens in Espronceda's poem. Parts I, II, III and IV in their formal present ordering do not correspond to the chronological narrative sequence.[6] The poem begins instead *in medias res*[7] where the strict chronological order should be read thusly: Parts II (Elvira's lament and death), III (Gambling den and Don Diego de Pastrana's challenge), I (Setting, Pastrana's death, and Don Félix's encounter with Elvira's ghost), IV (Don Félix' pursuit of Ghost and his own death).[8] Equally subjective, and reminiscent—from the vantage point of today's readers though not, needless to say, from the poet's—of Bergson's *durée réele* (psychological or interior time as opposed to time measured by the clock) is the treatment of time within the work itself.

The poem begins past the hour of midnight (v. 1: «Era más de medianoche...») on a Saturday and ends with the dawn of the next day (v. 1684: «...al naciente día...»). Less than twelve hours are spanned and yet it seems as if the action takes much longer. Time is stretched and shrunk in a surrealist fashion that further increases the confusion in the mind of the reader. Parts I, II and III all combined last much less than Part IV. It has more than double the number of verses of the other three put together, yet in reality more happens in the three initial segments. One of the few writers of the Generation of 1898 who admired Espronceda, Ramón del Valle Inclán, may have been close to the truth when in a piece written by Juan Ramón Jiménez he is quoted as saying that as far as he, Valle, is concerned in *El Estudiante de Salamanca* Picasso is already there to be found.' Meaning, I take it, a cubist reordering of reality.

El Estudiante de Salamanca is truly a poem of darkness and death because, as mentioned above, it takes place during the short night when witches gather (v. 19-20: «que los sábados convoca/ a las brujas a su fiesta») and also because all protagonists die at each other's hands. Elvira dies on account of Don Félix' disdain for her; Don Diego dies killed by Don Félix' sword; Don Félix is mortally wounded by Don Diego in their duel and is finally crushed to death by a skeletal Elvira whom he had caused to die at the beginning. A circle of death, so to speak.

In spite of this seemingly circular, kaleidoscopic or fragmentary ordering of events, the larger narrative structure of the poem is a journey—the symbolic journey of Don Félix through life which becomes a hallucinating chase ending in death. The essentially linear structure of the voyage through life corresponding to the *topos homo viator* is quite real: from Homer's *Odyssey,* a journey through land and sea, through Cervantes' *Don Quijote,* travels across La Mancha, to Melville's *Moby Dick*, the journey through the oceans in search of the White Whale. Espronceda, then, provides the reader in his poem with a view of the romantic concept of the universe that, as seen earlier in Chapter Two, has no absolutes which man can hold onto or believe in. Discredited are an ordered universe, the preeminence of reason over sentiment and the certainty of God's existence. In their place dynamism—meaning constant and inevitable change—and what the Romantics labelled Fate—meaning the unexplainable or unfathomable future—install themselves as the only coordinates of life.

IV. The Poem (*El Estudiante de Salamanca*) Itself

The four parts that structurally comprise *El Estudiante de Salamanca* can be integrated into two larger divisions. The first of these incorporates Parts I, II and III with the second composed solely of Part IV. There are several valid reasons for this grouping. The three inaugural parts of the poem transpire in an ambient of reality where the senses can be relied upon to ascertain the nature of events and to interpret the value of words spoken. In Part IV the world the reader perceives is more like an oneiric vision where sensations are distorted basically by the unknown quantities that are Death and the Dead, Hell and the Devil. Futhermore Parts I, II and III barely account in terms of lines (690 lines versus 1,012 in Part IV) for half of the poem, and reflect less interior or psychological time. We are dealing essentially with two very different halves: Parts I, II and III correspond to the life of Don Félix; Part IV to the nightmarish agony and death of the hero.

Part I contains, in its 179 verses, three distinct segments in this order: the setting of the crime, a portrayal of Don Félix and a portrayal of Doña Elvira. The action is set in the University city of Salamanca late one Saturday night. Both the night hours and the precise geographic location are characteristic of all romantic literature, not only in Espronceda's generation but also as late as Bécquer who in his *Leyendas* followed the same procedure—e.g., the city of Toledo in «El beso,» «La rosa de pasión,» «La voz del silencio,» «El Cristo de la calavera,» «Tres fechas,» «La ajorca de oro.» These writers relied on the absence of light to carry out whatever transformation these «familiar» localities needed for their purpose, therefore most climactic scenes take place either at dusk or at night, whether starry or moonless, and almost never in the light of a full sun. A moonless darkness populated by wandering souls, congregating witches, howling dogs, and bells that toll amidst the whistling of the wind serves as the stage for a duel in the shadows where a man loses his life to the infamous student Don Félix de Montemar. His fight won in the narrow, pitch-black *Calle del Ataúd,*[10] Don Félix hurries past an image of Christ, whose lamp, the only light in the street, reflects on the still bloody sword that took Don Diego de Pastrana's life. The portrait of this fearless rake is of a man whose life is given to womanizing, gambling, dueling, drinking and irreverence—vices that in the eyes of most can be dismissed on account of his bravery, generosity, wealth, good looks and noble birth:

Que en su arrogancia y sus vicios,
Caballeresca apostura,
agilidad y bravura
ninguno alcanza a igualar:

Que hasta en sus crímenes mismos,
en su impiedad y altiveza,
pone un sello de grandeza
don Félix de Montemar. (v. 132-139)

Whereas the satanic Don Félix' characterization appears in the rapid *octavilla aguda* seen above, Doña Elvira's contrasting portrait—«angel puro,» «inocente y desdichada»—comes to us in the paused verse of the *octava real*. She is seen only through her love for Don Félix who preyed on her vulnerable innocence, her candor, and her illusions; not a match for the guile and the duplicity of a calloused seducer for whom love was simply a game. Elvira's portrait emphasizes her eyes. On them the poet dwells both in the first—v. 141: «...dulces ojos lánguidos y hermosos»—*octava real* strophe and in the last one—v. 174-175: «...los ojos de ella/ astros de gloria, manantial de vida»—having them reveal not only an attractive physical beauty but also a measure of the spiritual radiance that moves her.

Part II, depicting Elvira's decline and death, begins with a lyrical interlude, a total contrast to the lugubrious opening scene of the poem in Part I. Nature here suggests an intimate form of poetry by way of a melancholy moon. In this idyllic setting a woman eventually appears, white and grieving. Elvira's love misfortune is revealed first by the poet from an external perspective that focuses solely on her, then the reader is taken into the poet's confidence, and finally the heroine herself speaks directly in a six *octava real* lament.

Apparent throughout Part II are Elvira's candid innocence, Nature's indifference to her plaint and the total devotion to Don Félix that has driven her to madness. The words «pure,» «virgin» and «candid,» the beginning of the frequent attribution of the adjective «white» and its derivatives to Elvira, and comparisons with the flowers of the garden where she wanders in this night portray her as the maiden whose innocence was lost to a deceiver infinitely more artful than she. Her payment for this irreparable loss resembles once again the fate of the acacia blossoms and the roses that surround her. Elvira's deflowering, like the rose's, amounts to her death, and her life thus parallels the flower's own.

...flor venturosa,
llena de amor murió de juventud:
Despertó alegre una alborada hermosa,
y a la tarde durmió en el ataúd. (v. 355-358)

Whereas Don Félix' motto seems to be «seize the day» (*carpe diem*), Elvira's fate is contained in the one that says «life is short» (*vita brevis*), both *topoi* more often associated with Renaissance literature than with Romanticism.

Equally well known is the literary habit of having a character regain his or her sanity prior to death. Don Quijote's remark to his friends, in Cervantes' masterpiece (*Don Quijote* II, 74), «en los nidos de antaño no hay pájaros hogaño,» is perhaps the best-known example of this deathbed transformation. Elvira sheds her madness long enough to pen a farewell letter to Don Félix and upon completing it, as though the effort had been too much for her, she dies in her mother's grasp muttering an inaudible name, which we assume to be her lover's. Aware that death's cold hand tugs at her, Elvira addresses herself to Don Félix for the last time. In these six stanzas (v. 371-418) Elvira manifests a love totally absent of any regrets (v. 386-394), an apology for having her love survive his and the resultant refusal on her part to give up hope (v. 394-400), and a confession of a love so complete that it wishes happiness for her lover and exculpates him from any blame (v. 403-410).

A change in versification from *octavas reales* to *cuartetos* signals the end of Elvira's direct voicing of her lament. She is once again viewed from the outside as she gives up her life seeking peace in the tomb, recalling the attitude of the poet in «A Jarifa en una orgía» who in typical romantic fashion had declared (v. 76): «Sólo en la paz de los sepulcros creo.»[11]

Part II once more follows literary canons when the heroine dies and the poem ends at sunset, simultaneously suggesting the end of the day (v. 433-434): «allá en la tarde, cuando el sol declina, / baña su tumba en paz su último rayo.» The falling branches of a funereal willow tree complete the melancholy portrait of the unlucky Elvira.

Part III, the last segment of the first division of *El Estudiante de Salamanca*, is unlike any other part of the poem. Though still written in verse form, its lines belong to a dialogue carried out among the eight characters that walk in and out of the four scenes. Part III's 257 verses, most of them asonantal *octosílabos* (save for Don Diego de Pastrana's presentation done in *endecasílabos*), are a throwback to the very popular Golden Age plays of *capa y espada* and indeed this Part could certainly pass for an Act in one of Lope de Vega's or one of his contemporaries' plays. Not that Espronceda was the first or even the last romantic author to draw so openly on Spanish Baroque theatre. The third act (scenes 1-4) of the Duke of Rivas' famous play *Don Alvaro o la fuerza del sino,* first staged on March 22, 1835, is a clear antecedent: a gambling hall filled with unsavory players and the presence of the hero as well as the heroine's brother. Nine years later after *Don Alvaro* and four after *El Estudiante de Salamanca,* Zorrilla's *Don Juan Tenorio* opens with a similar scene at the Laurel Tavern.

Prior to Scene 1 Espronceda sets the stage with five short stanzas. Here the six gamblers appear as unrepentant addicts bent only on winning and betting at cards. The room, barely lit by a dim lamp, its walls darkened by smoke, is characterized as «infernal.» Its windows can scarcely contain the force of a violent storm outside that pounds the glass as though it were the wings of a giant bird. When Scene 1 finally opens we see the six anonymous card players arguing amongst themselves, cursing their luck and alluding to Don Félix' generosity in connection with a loan to the First Gambler. As it turns out later (Scene 2, v. 532) this player's name is Don Juan—the significance of the onomastic characterization and its connection with Don Félix should not be overlooked—but he is the only one thus identified, the rest characterize themselves through action and dialogue. Thus the First Gambler's name is Don Juan, a friend of Don Félix and the big loser in the game; the Third Gambler is the big winner; the Second Gambler and the Fifth prop up the dialogue; the Fourth Gambler hates Don Félix (v. 692: «Me alegraré que lo mate,») although we don't know why; and the Sixth Gambler never does or says anything.

Don Félix having been alluded to—a dramatic ploy that piques the audience's curiosity to discover what the named character is really like—now makes his entrance at the beginning of Scene 2. The attractiveness of his male presence is once more extolled (v. 467-474) but in a deliberate, studied contrast to that of Don Diego who will, in turn, open Scene 3. Don Félix, hat tilted back on his head, enters decidedly and is welcomed by his cronies. What follows in this scene is a first hand look at Don Félix who now speaks openly and face-to-face with other men. The reader perceives him as a despicable character, not so much because of his penchant for gambling, but because of his willingness to put on the table as security for his bets not only Elvira's jeweled locket and her miniature portrait but even the girl herself had she been there. This desecration of her memory—the fact that Don Félix ignores her death does nothing to diminish his reproachable actions since after learning of it he remains totally unaffected—lowers the esteem of the protagonist immeasurably. His giving of himself to the Devil several times over, though not unnatural in these surroundings, becomes highly signficant once we are to learn what follows in Part IV.

Scene 3 parallels the preceeding one in an antithetical fashion. We remember Don Félix entering as an imposing, virile, swaggering figure, hand on the hilt of his sword, hat back on his head. Don Diego, on the other hand, comes in noiselessly, his body and face hidden by cape and hat to such a degree that even Don Félix, engrossed as he is in the game, remarks: «entre el sombrero y la capa/ se os ve apenas la nariz.» (v. 582-583). The insolent tone of such a greeting is sustained by Don Félix through the whole scene. Moreover, Don Félix' either pretended or genuine interest in the cards makes a mockery of Don Diego's avowed resolve to avenge his sister's death by killing her cruel lover. That Pastrana has journeyed from far-away Flanders, that Elvira has died through his fault or that Don Diego seeks to cleanse his family's honor by a duel leaves Don Félix indifferent. He continues betting, counting his winnings, sarcastically replying to his inquisitor (v. 679-680) «no se mueren de amor / las mujeres de hoy en día»—parodying the prototypical romantic heroine— until he finally relents and good naturedly, though still totally disinterested, consents to crossing swords with Don Diego, suggesting that the whole affair is not worth getting killed for. [12]

The fourth and last scene, a mere eight verses long, protagonized by the gamblers, simply sets the stage for the duel between the two men which had already taken place in Part I and is recalled at the very beginning of Part IV. As will be remembered, contrary to what the Fourth Gambler had hoped, Don Diego dies at the hands of Don Félix, who nevertheless is himself fatally wounded by his victim.

After the references to the imminent duel that close Part III, Don Félix can be seen walking away from *Ataúd* Street having just disposed of Doña Elvira's brother. This sight reiterates and magnifies the crossing of swords accompanied by a blood-curdling scream that took place in Part I (v. 41-48). Such are the opening stanzas of Part IV, the longest (1,012 verses) and most arcane segment of *El Estudiante de Salamanca*. But although it seems to be the longest part in terms of time elapsed, a notion reinforced by more, and often longer, verse lines than the other three parts combined, in essence it must be the shortest since it takes place between the hour Don Félix is mortally wounded by Don Diego and the moment he dies. [13] The whole fourth part of the poem, then, constitutes the protagonist's agony—moments before his death.

There are only three recognizable stages in this terminal struggle whose outcome only Don Félix can ignore. Uncertainty and delirium make up the first state. Here Don Félix beholds the presence of a mysterious ethereal woman, initially revealed by a sigh and then more closely outlined as a figure kneeling before the dimly lighted image of Christ on Casket Street. With this supernatural apparition begins a chase that constitutes the core of the indicated first stage. Don Félix embarks upon the pursuit of a white (always this same adjective), elusive and nearly silent woman-like Ghost. He finds, however, that the more he advances toward the Ghost, the further it retreats from him—Don Félix cannot touch it. Realizing that he is not vinous—v. 737-738: «Mas el vapor del néctar jerezano / nunca su mente a transtornar bastara»—Don Félix blasphemes, invoking the Devil when his will power no longer suffices to control the situation. Buildings shake, streets ondulate and the fleeting figure is given chase through now-familiar, now-unrecognizable, Salamancan neighborhoods. Striving to gain her attention, Don Félix finally succeeds in making the Ghost speak, and though it is only to warn him of the danger involved in his obstinacy, Montemar considers this breaking of silence a major victory. What with her beauty, her growing warmth, her knowledge of his name when he ignores hers, the propitiousness of darkness and their situation alone, Don Félix dismisses as nonsense the Ghost's repeated warnings of the peril he runs. Thus when the Ghost exclaims «¡Cúmplase en fin tu voluntad, Dios mío!» in verse 939, at last the reader knows that Don Félix' soul is irretrievably lost; there's no turning back. The utterance more than suggests a pact made by Elvira with God to try and save the protagonist from Hell—one last chance to resist temptation and thus redeem himself. When he does not show contrition of any kind, however, Elvira's soul is condemned along with his.[14]

A storm of apocalyptic proportions marks the beginning of the second stage, the hallucinatory vision of his own and Don Diego's funeral. Phrases applied to Don Félix such as he «begins to confuse,» «to get lost,» «to ignore where he walks,» «to determine where he is,» and allusions to «the Beyond» and to the «endless Voyage» as well as a vocabulary that monotonously repeats «funereal,» «sepulchral,» «languid,» «moribund,» and «spectral» all conduct the protagonist toward his end. The reader no longer feels surprise at encountering scores of skeletons in a *danse macabre* to the tolling of bells nor the shock or anger the hero himself feels when he contemplates his body and Don Diego's in their respective coffins on their way to the graveyard for burial. And yet Montemar, perversely grandiose in his defiance of God, maintains his characteristic insolence humming a drinking song (v. 1261: «Un báquico cantar tarareando.») while his white Ghost leads him, Beatrice-like, through an immensely tall gate and along a vast subterranean passage that seems to have no end. Once deep into the house of death, the third stage of Don Félix' journey commences, characterized by a vertiginous tempo appropriately enough begun by Montemar's fall down a seemingly endless black marble spiral staircase. At his landing, there awaits a nuptial bed that looks strangely like a sepulchre, a terrifying din made by the gnashing of teeth and the crushing of bones, and the presence of two distinct figures who expect him to join them. In a macabre scene Don Félix' marriage to Doña Elvira, witnessed by a still bleeding Don Diego, takes place and the conclusion of the poem now parallels Don Félix own end. The kissing of the bride, a repulsive scene where Elvira's fleshless and rotting skeleton first caresses and ultimately crushes the life out of Don Félix in an infernal embrace, signals the last gasp for Montemar. The progressively shorter and weakened breaths are echoed in the equally diminishing verses that descend to the one syllable «*son*» («beat») which we take to mean Don Félix' last. This recrudescent death of the unrepentant hero at the hands of his victims, seen in terms of an oneiric darkness, contrasts with the dawning light of a new day as if one were awakening from a frightful nightmare.

V. History and Sources of *El Diablo Mundo*

Though more pages have been written by 20th century critics about *El Diablo Mundo* than almost all other Espronceda works, few of us remember anything more about this long poem (over 6,000 verses) except for its second canto, «Canto a Teresa» (see Chapter Five), which ironically enough, as will be recalled, the poet advises can be skipped since it has little to do with the remainder of the work. However, Espronceda and his publisher must have thought that *El Diablo Mundo* would have wide appeal and set out to enhance its chances with the public by selling it in serialized form, much in the fashion of the novels by Fernández y González and other feuilleton authors of that time. The first issue was published in July 1840 by the bookseller and printer Ignacio Boix in Madrid. It contained the «Prólogo» by Antonio Ros de Olano[15] and the «Introducción.» Subsequent issues contained the six cantos at the rate of one per installment. After the third issue, containing the second canto, a fragment acknowledged to be from *El Diablo Mundo* titled «El angel y el poeta» appeared in the magazine *El Iris* on February 7, 1841. This piece, as F. Caravaca[16] and R. Marrast[17] previously have suggested, seems to be closely related to the «Introducción» and/or the first canto. In no way does it advance the narrative beyond either of these two segments, and no modern edition of *El Diablo Mundo* inserts it directly into any sequence within the poem, but rather it is made to appear after the unfinished seventh canto. Probably shortly thereafter this princeps edition became extremely rare[18] so that the one on which all later editions are based was done, also by the Boix Company, in 1841 as a two-volume work.

Both the mid-nineteenth century's and today's readers are immediately struck by several things about *El Diablo Mundo*. Foremost undoubtedly has to be the poet's declared purpose to chronicle minutely the whole of humanity's course,

> Nada menos te ofrezco que un Poema
> con lances raros y revuelto asunto,
> de nuestro mundo y sociedad emblema,
> que hemos de recorrer punto por punto.
> Si logro yo desenvolver mi tema,
> fiel traslado ha de ser, cierto trasunto
> de la vida del hombre y la quimera
> tras de que va la humanidad entera. (v. 1356-1363)

a pledge so ambitious that it couldn't but fall short.

Secondly, one is at awe of Espronceda's unprecedented practice of publishing his epic of the human race in installments. Very obviously there is no lack of self-confidence in his inspiration, heuristic gifts, or the largeness of the chosen theme. And finally, the poet's virtuosity in carrying out his promise for more than six thousand verse-lines ranging from the easy flowing *quintillas* to the solemn and very difficult *octavas reales* continues to impress even those most widely read, especially considering that only Espronceda's death put an end to *El Diablo Mundo.* [19]

Espronceda's attempt has no forerunner in Spanish literature, though it is not difficult to conjecture that what had occupied the minds of other European writers of the post-Rousseau era concerned him equally. Goethe's *Faust,* his masterpiece work where the protagonist scholar makes a pact with Mephistopheles in his study room, reminds us of the rejuvenation of Espronceda's personaje. [20] Much the same could be said of Lord Byron's *Manfred* and his *Don Juan.* [21] But Espronceda's poem remains uniquely his, partially in the sense that it reflects a rebellious, disorganized and pessimistic attitude. This translates into a fragmented, digressionary and often improvised, though inspired, major work that can be dismissed, as some do, by merely salvaging its second Canto, «A Teresa. Descansa en Paz.» Indeed the critical consensus is that in spite of all of its cited imperfections, or perhaps because of them since they are so typically Esproncedian, *El Diablo Mundo* must be considered the paradigm of this Spanish Romantic at his most characteristic.

The poem failed in part because of its grand scheme and, of course, because the death of its author cut it short,²³ though it is difficult to see from the seven remaining Cantos how the frequent digressions, the mixture of lyricism, satire, discourse, dialogue and narrative, the alternating of verse forms or the improvisatory nature of a composition issued in installments could have been remedied by its completion. True, Espronceda might have finished it, but as far as the Romantics were concerned that would not have endowed the work with any greater virtue. For them a fragment per se was as viable a structure as that of any other literary genre.²⁴ More objectionable perhaps was *El Diablo Mundo*'s failure to achieve the universality promised at its outset, never reaching beyond the confines of a Spain, almost exclusively Madrid, that by topography and chronology we know to be precisely that of the 1840s. Whether Espronceda could or would have progressed from such confines of the particular to a more universalized stage we can never know since a complete outline of the poem never existed and we do not know how many Cantos it was to eventually number and, thus, how much unfolding of the story line is represented by the seven that we do have.

VI. The Poem (*El Diablo Mundo*) Itself

The «Introducción,» a 651-verse series of ninety-seven strophes, sets the stage as the Poet, lost in thought, suddenly becomes aware of a chorus of demons shattering the silence of nighttime. The din increases while, in a rapid cadence versification, an apocalyptic vision that includes nothing but the most horrifying sounds of war, tempests, orgies, animal and human screams takes over the whole scenario. It is as though the forces of evil, through this Babel, have conspired to take over the world and make it into their own kingdoms. The likelihood of their success becomes evident when a colossal Lucifer rises out of an abyss of blackness and fire, lording over swarms of minions that await his commands. Evil appears to be so powerful and pervasive that man has little chance to escape it. In fact it seems inevitable that the Devil, not God, shall control the world.²⁵ Thus this satanic vision that excludes any chance for human happiness and instead sows endless doubt, despair and suffering will serve as the constant background for the whole of *El Diablo Mundo*.

The Canto I (verses 652-1499) likewise written in various meters, incorporates *octavillas, serventesios, quintillas,* and *octavas reales.* The scene opens in a small, soberly furnished room where a man is seated at a pine table reading a book by the light of an oil lamp. As a nearby clock strikes twelve o'clock midnight, the man, very old and very tired, closes the book he has been studying and ponders the essence of life. It occurs to him that vanity, madness and mendacity pretty much sum up his feelings toward the world as a man who knows that, his youth having been spent, little remains for him except to die. Life's mystery has not revealed itself to him in spite of all the years gone by. Feeling deceived he guesses that only by «being forever young and immortal» (v. 701: «ser para siempre joven e inmortal») could man ever hope to be happy and have no regrets; but, alas, everything must perish, and he expects only more of this madness he recognizes as part of life. Disconsolate, the old man yields to fatigue and falls asleep. In his slumber two beautiful women pay him a visit. They are Death and Life, who, in two of the most striking chants, seek in turn to convince Pablo to do as each proposes. Death invites him to the peace and eternal quiet that awaits after a life of toil and uncertainty. Her powers of persuasion are such that he is about to surrender his tired and defeated self unto Death when Life bursts in to forestall such an arrangement. Instead, surrounded by the power of singing angels, winds and lights, Life turns the tide by offering Pablo another alternative, one he had hours before only dreamed could exist: immortality. It is a choice he makes only too willingly, and one whose results are not long in coming. He has hardly reached with his hands for those stretched out to him by Life when

> sienten grato calor sus miembros muertos,
> con nuevo ardor su corazón palpita.
>
> La sangre hierve en las hinchadas venas,
> siente volver los juveniles bríos,
> y ahuyentan de su frente albas serenas
> los pensamientos de la edad sombríos. (v. 1198-1204)

The whole Canto I has not been an uninterrupted unfolding of the foregoing. On the contrary, interspersed throughout the mainstream of the narrative are many digressions. These, though they may detract from the linear continuity of the poem, offer us an encyclopedic account of the poet's ruminations. Espronceda interrupts his tale to tell about his enemies (the Count of Toreno), the purpose of this composition as he envisions it, the time of his writing it, and his feelings about a multitude of things. This is a practice that will continue throughout *El Diablo Mundo* and which, although exasperating and distracting at times, lends it a personal immediacy and an individuality difficult to dismiss.

The Canto II, the famous «A Teresa. Descanse en paz» amounts to the

poem's grandest digression. As already noted, the Canto II has little or
nothing to do with *El Diablo Mundo*. Completely autonomous, «A
Teresa» can stand on its own, just as *El Diablo Mundo* can be read without
it. As it will be remembered, Espronceda appended a footnote to its title
suggesting that very course to the reader.[16] There can be little doubt at this
point that the poet, pressured by the constant deadlines imposed by the installment form of the publication and not having finished the next Canto,
chose to insert instead this magnificent forty-four *octava real* elegy. Unsur-
passed in the genre in Spanish literature since Espronceda, it was written
soon after Teresa's death for what some critics have felt may have been
«therepeutic reasons, sacrificing his art to his need for spiritual health.»[17]

The Canto III (verses 1820-3020) half written in *silvas* and half in *octavas reales*, begins with a lament for the fleeting nature of time. Quoting
Horace, this *tempus fugit topos* ties in with the melancholy regrets voiced
in the Canto I by the old man Pablo who missed the joys of youth so keenly
in his waning years. However, the sadness of this backward glance does not
last or reach the point of disillusion witnessed in the earlier Canto; instead,
the spectacle of a joyous spring morning takes over the tenor of the verses.
Spring, traditional season of rebirth, brings with it the rejuvenation of
Pablo who, now vigorous and childlike, is renamed Adán. Adán, even
though a throwback to Pablo's youth, is completely dispossessed of any
knowledge of the world. His innocence, ignorance and inexperience are
totally unlike Goethe's Faust who, in addition to his newly acquired
powers, could count on his years lived as a mere mortal. The contrast,
then, that this young, beautiful and trusting human being offers when compared to the people surrounding him gives Espronceda ample opportunity
to employ his pen in a savage diatribe against the prejudice, duplicity and
inhumanity of civilized man. As a result of Adán's nakedness, this
«newborn» youth is ridiculed and put in jail evincing, in the poet's eyes, a
socio-political hypocrisy based on conventionalisms that leave no room for
justice or compassion. Consequently, the digressions toward the end of this
Canto III paint a dismal picture of nineteenth century Spanish society, its
decayed mores and its characteristic baseness. Verses 2573-2932 are no less
striking, in their portrayal of the Madrid populace as nothing but unfeeling
riffraff, than Goya's vivid canvasses of the same theme. This bitter note on
which the third Canto ends contrasts sharply with the dawning of a new life
so hopefully presented at the beginning with the coming of Spring—a continuing and relentless disillusionment that pervades life in *El Diablo Mundo*.

The Canto IV (verses 3021-4076), done in its entirety in *octavas reales*
save for Tío Lucas' pronouncement in *redondillas,* continues with two

minor digressions at the beginning and at the end of this segment to recount
Adán's saga in the civilized world. He has been imprisoned now for one
year and his schooling into the ways of the underworld has begun, tutored
by a sage in such matters whose name is Tío Lucas. This likeable and accomplished criminal protects and instructs Adán who, in his still semi-
virginal innocence, fails to comprehend the ways of the world. A visitor to
Tío Lucas, his daughter Salada, causes Adán to experience for the first time
what falling in love means in a curious parallel with Espronceda's own life
when he was a prisoner in one of Lisbon's jails. There he had befriended
Colonel Epifanio Mancha and through him his daughter Teresa, the most
important woman in Espronceda's life and poetry. Salada, a prostitute, as
Teresa would some day become, returns Adán's passion and cares for him
in deeds and words until she succeeds in securing his release from prison.
Together they find an apartment in the Arapiés neighborhood. As the Canto IV ends, Adán and Salada engage in amorous pastimes which represent
the only prolonged moments of happiness for either character, or for any
other, in the whole poem. Momentarily, love has saved Adán from a life in
prison and has won the day for him, staving off the inevitable.

Canto V (verses 4077-4983), a dramatic mini-play divided into two
acts, is written in *redondillas* in the first and octosyllabic *romances* and
serventesios in the second. *Cuadro* I takes place in an Arapiés
neighborhood tavern where Adán and Salada drink and converse while
others in the room, most of them local truants, carry on loudly with songs
and accompanying guitar music. Salada's amorous urgings are not sufficient to hold Adán's attention which drifts to a group at a nearby table
presided over by a defrocked priest. Adán's head is still swimming with the
visions of wealth, power and riches that, he now knows from Lucas'
larcenous advice, the upper class nobility possess and that he himself would
like to enjoy. When the group's songs turn into insults directed at the two
lovers, a quarrel ensues and the melee ends with the stabbing death of one
of Salada's ex-lovers by her own hand. *Cuadro* II, twice as long as the first
one, is in turn divided into two small scenes, both set in the home of Adán
and Salada. In the first the two are alone, dialoguing in a fashion similar to
their earlier conversation at the bar. In the course of this exchange Adán
falls asleep in his lover's arms, and upon awakening relates his dream of
gold, beauty and pleasures. Salada's reaction to all of Adán's fantasies
amounts to a saddened resignation that her devoted love for Adán is not
enough to satisfy or hold him. He no longer returns Salada's passion, but
instead feels shackled by it. A combination of her devotion and the en-
thusiastic madness with which Adán single-mindedly pursues his hunger for
wealth enlist Salada's interest. With the coming of the second scene we

witness the arrival of the priest and several other thieves who in Adán's presence plan to rob the mansion of a wealthy woman of the nobility. As Adán listens carefully to the discussion his interst grows with the mention of the great booty to be had from the robbery. Not fully aware of the implications involved in the taking of someone else's property and breaking into another's home, Adán eagerly joins the band of thieves, brutally casting aside a weeping Salada who begs him desperately but unsuccessfully to disengage himself from such a criminal and dangerous enterprise. This is the last time Salada appears in the poem as Adán, throwing off her arms, leads the robbers out the door.

The Canto VI (verses 4985-5805), unlike those before it, contains almost no digressions. The stroke of one o'clock in the morning marks its beginning, a calm moonlit spring night in which the sounds of dancing and celebrating fill the air. As the poet's focus narrows, the vision shifts initially to an upper-class neighborhood and then closes in upon an impressive mansion, home of the Countess of Alcira. Following a white moonbeam through a half-opened balcony window, we enter the palace and behold the same sight that moments later will stun Adán. In a sumptuous bedroom of damask curtains, silk sheets, gleaming mirrors and perfumed gowns sleeps the beautiful Countess. Adán, amazed at the richness and beauty of the room lets his cohorts ransack it while he marvels at the wonder of it all. The sight of his own face and body reflected in a mirror (verses 5162-5179) holds the same charming and innocent narcissism as that of a child who for the first time realizes he is looking at his own image. Unfortunately, as Adán toys with a magnificent mantel clock, its chimes go off, the sleeping figure awakens and, startled, cries out for help. Interrupted in their pillaging, the thieves decide to silence the woman with a knife. Adán, however, taken with her helpless beauty turns against his accomplices and defends the Countess. Thus foiled and alarmed by the warning voice «¡La justicia!», the thieves and Adán—remembering that the word meant jail the last time he heard it—run out of the mansion and scatter in the night, disappearing into the darkness of the Madrid streets. As Casalduero writes,[28] the bandits who earlier caused Adán to abandon Salada now force him to do the same with the Countess of Alcira. The longer Adán's tenure in the world becomes, the less immune he becomes to the tribulations and disillusionments that affect all men. Wandering aimlessly through the streets, Adán hears the sounds and music that he realizes are coming from a house of prostitution. As he nears the bordello Adán notices an open window in an adjoining building. Upon approaching he sees there laying in state the body of a young woman whose mother, María, wailing at her death, damns God's cruel mercilessness. Confronted with the reality of death only for the first time, its impact on Adán is yet tinged with an innocence that stems from his belief in a benevolent God.[29] The contrast between the grieving mother in this funeral scene and the sounds of laughter and drinking heard from the brothel next door underscore the ultimate despair and alienation of those most stricken with pain. It will be remembered from Chapter Four that the protagonist of «El reo de muerte» underwent a similar fate. The noise and the laughter of partygoers that kept him awake on the night of his execution accented equally his loneliness and man's inhumanity toward his fellowman. And though he here calls her Lucía, Espronceda was still very much thinking of his beloved Teresa, already dead and sung in the famous Canto II «A Teresa. Descanse en Paz». These lines,

> vio con sorpresa que a calmar no atina
> de par en par abierta una ventana,
> y en una estancia solitaria y triste,
> entre dos hachas de amarilla cera
> un fúnebre ataúd, y en él tendida
> una joven sin vida
> que aun en la muerte interesante era. (v. 5427-5434)

recall the events of the night of September 18, 1839, when the poet, walking to his apartment after leaving a dinner party, saw Teresa's casket through an open window in the lower floor of 22 Santa Isabel Street.[30] It was a vision that haunted Espronceda for the rest of his life.

Canto VII, comprised of fourteen *octavas* and published posthumously by the poet's friend Miguel de los Santos Alvarez who later tried to write a continuation to *El Diablo Mundo*[31] amounts to little over two fragments. Written in an elegiac vein, they are sung by the old woman María, the bereaved mother of the previous canto who vents her grief to Adán in the first, while consoling herself with the happy memories of Lucía's childhood in the second. For all practical purposes, it can be said that *El Diablo Mundo* ends with the final stanza of the sixth canto.

«El angel y el poeta,» as mentioned earlier, is a disconnected fragment of the poem initially published on February 7, 1841, in *El Iris* of Madrid printed separately though it appears tenuously related to the «Introducción» or the Canto VII. Written in *silvas* and in dialogue form between the Poet and an Angel, this one hundred and one verse fragment represents Espronceda's highest exaltation of the Poet as an all-seeing, all-knowing thaumaturg. This rebellious deification of the myth-making function that the poet embodies according to Espronceda, vaguely reminiscent of Don

Félix de Montemar's defiance of God, is challenged by the Angel who brands the Poet a cainite that should rise above material things if indeed he is endowed with power, knowledge and vision superior to the rest of men. «The Angel and the Poet» is a panegyric to the role and the persona of the poet seldom more inspired or idolatrous.

In *El Diablo Mundo* Espronceda maintains to the last his attitude, seen earlier in the «Canciones» cycle (Chapter Four), that man lives surrounded by an evil that he cannot defeat or even escape. Most of his heroes up to this point—the pirate, the beggar, the executioner, the condemned man, even Don Félix de Montemar to a certain degree, and now Adán—have been singular individuals unable to cope with life in a full social context. All are outcasts, not by choice but as a result of their inability to cope with the greed, mendacity, hypocrisy and other incarnations of evil in civilization. Adán, in *El Diablo Mundo,* personifies a Noble Savage in the Rousseaunian sense who precisely because of his candor and lack of guile cannot survive in a world populated by other men whose patina of civilization endows them with arms for survival—i.e., duplicity, deceit, etc. In a sense, *El Diablo Mundo* is a thesis poem, one so large and so full of digressions that, in addition to its admirable lyrical passages, it creates a situation made to demonstrate its author's contention: the world as it stands is no place for man. Once again Espronceda's romantic expectations by far exceed reality's possibilities.

NOTES

1. Robert Marrast, *José de Espronceda et son temps* (Paris, 1874), pp. 668-69.

2. Elías Torre, «García de Villalta y Espronceda. Un inmediato antecedente de 'El estudiante de Salamanca',» *Insula*, 132 (November 1957), n.p.

3. Marrast, *op. cit.,* pp. 645-66.

4. Russell P. Sebold, «El infernal arcano de Félix de Montemar,» *Hispanic Review,* 46 (Autumn 1978), 456.

5. Joaquín Casalduero, *Espronceda* (Madrid, 1967), p. 184.

6. David William Foster, «A Note on Espronceda's use of the Romance Meter in *El Estudiante de Salamanca,»* *Romance Notes,* 7 (1965), 2-3.

7. Casalduero, *op. cit.,* p. 205.

8. All major critics (Allen, Casalduero, Hutman, Varela Jácome, Foster), except for Marrast, believe, as I do, that Espronceda, aware or not of his vanguardist chronological technique succeeded in a temporal fragmentation concordant with the chaotic meaning of this poem.

9.   Juan Ramón Jiménez, «Ramón del Valle-Inclán (Castillo de quema),» in his *Páginas escojidas (Prosa)* (Madrid: Gredos, 1958), p. 137.

10.   In fact this street exists not only in Sevilla as told in the previously cited Mañara books but also in Salamanca. Equally meaningful characterization is «Monte/mar» (Mountain/Sea), suggesting a universal evilness in the protagonist.

11.   Casalduero, *op. cit.*, p. 192.

12.   In Rivas' play, Don Alvaro is equally reluctant to fight Leonor's brothers though this hero's reason is that he believes more than enough blood has been shed already. Don Félix, on the other hand, simply does not think a duel is warranted and he does not want to be bothered with anything that will distract him from his winning streak.

13.   Norma Louise Hutmann, «Don círculos en la niebla: 'El estudiante de Salamanca' y 'El diablo mundo',» *Papeles de Son Armadans,* 59 (October 1970), 13.

14.   A pact with similar provisos, it will be remembered, was struck with God by Doña Inés who does succeed in saving her Don Juan Tenorio in Zorrilla's play.

15.   A close friend of Espronceda to whom the poet dedicated this work.

16.   Francisco Caravaca, «Espronceda y el mundo caótico de *El diablo mundo,*» *Les Langues Néo-Latines,* 172 (March-April 1965), 41-59.

17.   Marrast, «Introducción» to *José de Espronceda: El Estudiante de Salamanca. El Diablo Mundo* (Madrid: Castalia, 1978), p. 43.

18.   *Ibid.,* p. 41.

19.   He penned the remaining verses of the seventh canto only days before succumbing to diphtheria.

20.   Alessandro Marinengo, «Espronceda ante la leyenda faústica,» *Revista de Literatura,* 57-58 (January-June 1966), 35-55.

21.   Américo Castro, «Acerca de *El Diablo Mundo,* de Espronceda, «*Revista de Filología Española,* 7 (1920), 374-78.

22.   Phillip Churchman, «Byron and Espronceda,» *Revue Hispanique,* 20 (1909), 167-98.

23.   Ironically it ends with a portrayal of a death (Lucia's) that no one doubts was patterned after Teresa's own.

24.   Hutman, *op. cit.,* pp. 7-8.

25.   Monroe Z. Hafter, «*El Diablo Mundo* in the Light of Carlyle's *Sartor Resartus,*» *Revista Hispánica Moderna,* 38 (1972-1973), 46.

26.   See Chapter V, footnote number 13.

27.   Bruce W. Wardropper, «Espronceda's *Canto a Teresa* and the Spanish Elegiac Tradition,» *Bulletin of Hispanic Studies,* 40 (1963), 89.

28.   Casalduero, *op. cit.,* p. 247.

29.   Hafter, *op. cit.,* p. 55.

30.   See Chapters I and V.

31.   In the magazine *Semanario pintoresco español* in 1853, Espronceda's friend, Miguel de los Santos Alvarez published a continuation of *El Diablo Mundo* along with eight unpublished *octavas* done by Espronceda before his death.

CHAPTER SEVEN

A Foray Into the Theater

None of the Romantics wrote exclusively for the stage; most considered themselves poets and primarily they were that, as well as novelists or essayists who also happened to write plays. Yet, in large measure, save perhaps for Espronceda, famous as a poet, or Larra, equally well known as a social essayist, it was through one or more plays that most of the romantic writers are best remembered: Francisco Martínez de la Rosa for his play *La conjuración de Venecia,* the Duke of Rivas for his *Don Alvaro o la fuerza del sino,* Antonio García Gutiérrez for his *El Trovador,* Juan Eugenio Hartzenbusch for his *Los amantes de Teruel,* and, of course, José Zorrilla for his *Don Juan Tenorio.*

It is not too surprising, then, that Espronceda gave in to the temptation of writing for the theater. Much as the post-romantic poet Gustavo Adolfo Bécquer was to do a quarter of a century later,[1] Espronceda had a career as a playwright in association with two collaborators, producing two dramas and one more play on his own. The results of these efforts are these dramas, *Ni el tío ni el sobrino, Amor venga sus agravios* and *Blanca de Borbón.* The first two were staged but enjoyed little or no success in Espronceda's lifetime, whereas the third one has yet to be put on the stage. Indeed, *Blanca de Borbón* was not even published until nearly thirty years after the author's death, and then in a very limited private edition by his daughter whose name, like the heroine's, was Blanca.[2]

I. Characteristics of Spanish Romantic Drama

Historical drama inspired and to a great extent markedly influenced romantic theater in Spain. Not the Greek tragedies or the Roman comedies,

which the Romantics managed to avoid completely,³ but the times of the
Middle Ages and the Crusades and even the bygone era of the Hapsburgs
appealed to these playwrights. Though their interest in historical themes is
demonstrable, most of them distorted, reinterpreted and otherwise bent
history to their own needs and purposes. History served the Romantics well
as a backdrop in that its chronological or situational distance allowed them
to present current social or individual conflicts with a large degree of im-
punity and subjectivity. As was the case in other genres heretofore seen,
such as poetry, the concerns that moved the Romantics remained the same,
they were just transferred to the stage: freedom in all of its manifold
manifestations, the individual as a lone being against the whole world, passion rather than reason as the guiding light to be followed. Everything was
personalized as the titles (*Macías, El Trovador, Don Alvaro, Don Juan
Tenorio, Los amantes de Teruel*) of the best known pieces show. Rights
and conflicts took on the form of recognizable individualized dilemmas
where the characters became entangled in complicated and overwrought
endeavors to solve them. Mysterious personnages of unknown ancestry,
rich, noble and, for the most part, aristocratic, protagonize romantic
dramas—the latter term a new designation that replaces the old ones of
comedy and *tragedy*. This blurring of the classical norm applies equally to
other well-adhered-to canons up to the 1830s. Plays were written in verse,
in prose and in some cases (e.g. *Don Alvaro*) in a mixture of both. No
longer were three acts the rule, some plays had two, such as Zorrilla's *El
puñal del godo* or as many as the seven that make up *Don Juan Tenorio* by
the same dramatist. Neither the unity of time nor those of space or action
concerned any of the Romantics unduly. They constructed their works in
the fashion that best suited their plots and the ideas or intentions they wished to convey to the audience.

   In Spain romantic drama came to the forefront rather slowly, more so
than poetry (even if, because it is the most pronouncedly social of all the
genres, its triumphs resounded more), remained there for a short period,
and then declined very rapidly. Edgar Allison Peers would have Spanish
romantic drama lasting scarcely three years, beginning in 1834 with
Martínez de la Rosa's *La conjuración de Venecia* and ending in 1837, the
year when, on January 19, *Los amantes de Teruel* by Hartzenbusch was put
on the stage.⁴ Perhaps Allison Peers' contention falls somewhat on the side
of briefness, but to think that romantic Spanish theater endured beyond a
decade is untenable. Zorrilla's immortal *Don Juan Tenorio*, staged at the
Teatro del Príncipe on March 28, 1844, surely signals the end of its
preeminence and the close of the decade begun by Martínez de la Rosa's
work.

Until April 22, 1834 when the first romantic play, *La conjuración de Venecia,* premiered, the theater in Spain had been in decline. Neoclassical tragedies, warmed-over moralizing plays, Golden Age readaptations and translations of French eighteenth-century melodramas made up the fare that theatergoers of the time had to choose from. The heavy hand of Fernando VII's censors, the forced exile of the most talented writers, and the monetary greed and dominance of publishers and directors have been blamed for the dearth of original works in the first quarter of the nineteenth century.[5] Then, too, the *épater le bourgeoise* attitude that characterizes most of romantic literature must have given pause to nascent dramatists as they reflected on what the public's reaction might be to the shocking and frenetic situations offered in the theater. It isn't difficult to visualize how the Madrid audiences responded when they were served up the murders, abductions, adulteries, conspiracies, briberies, and sacrilege of, say, *Don Alvaro* or *Don Juan Tenorio,* having been accustomed to the mild moralities of Quintana and Moratín or the farcical banalities of Italian operettas popular in those days.

II. Situation of the Spanish Theater in the 1830s

That romantic theater triumphed even briefly in Spain can be ascribed in part to a keenly felt ennui. People were tired of the old rehashes and demanded new entertainment. Equally obvious are other attendant factors, difficulties which most romantic dramatists, along with all the rest who made their living writing for the stage, had to overcome—especially when judging from the following account by Fernando Fernández de Córdoba, an eloquent witness to the situation prevalent in most of the theaters in Madrid at the time. From Fernández de Córdoba's book, *Mis memorias íntimas,* Ricardo Navas Ruiz[6] cites this passage:

Luces macilentas de aceite que lo dejaban todo en penumbra y despedían un olor insoportable; palcos estrechísimos, mal pintados, mal decorados y pésimamente amueblados, a los cuales no podían asistir las damas con vestidos medianamente ricos por temor de mancharlos con polvo y aceite; una cazuela destinada exclusivamente a los señores, con sólo bancos de madera sin respaldo, sobre los cuales cada uno ponía almohadones expresamente traídos para este objeto de su casa; lunetas de tafilete, rotas, mugrientas y desvencijadas, cuando no totalmente reventadas y descubriendo el pelote; ...densa y constante atmósfera de humo; frío en el invierno hasta el punto de que los espectadores asistieran a la representación cuidadosamente envueltos en sus capas; calor asfixiante en verano por la falta de ventilaciones conventientes; empleados y acomodadores groseros que había que tratar a bastonazos hartas veces, y como complemento de este cuadro, un público medianamente culto todavía, cuyas manifestaciones eran violentísimas siempre.

Madrid had half a dozen theaters during those years described so dismally by Fernández de Córdoba. The two most important ones were the Teatro del Príncipe (now called Teatro Español) and the Teatro de la Cruz (Teatro del Drama as of 1849). Both were rather large, with a seating capacity of 1,200 for the Teatro del Príncipe and somewhere around 1,500 for the Teatro de la Cruz.[7] Of the two, the most prestigious was the Teatro del Príncipe where *Macías, Don Alvaro, El Trovador* and *Don Juan Tenorio* all had their premieres.

All of the representative romantic dramas are, without exception, largely historical, which is to say legendary. In the ten years (1834-1844) spanned by the romantics' theater, only six plays merit the label of masterpieces—Espronceda did not author any of them. They were: *La conjuración de Venecia* by Francisco Martínez de la Rosa, staged at the Teatro de la Cruz on April 22, 1834; *Macías* by Mariano José de Larra, staged at the Teatro del Príncipe on September 24, 1834; *Don Alvaro o la fuerza del sino* by the Duke of Rivas, staged at the Teatro del Príncipe on March 22, 1835; *El Trovador* by Antonio García Gutiérrez, staged at the Teatro del Príncipe on March 1, 1836; *Los amantes de Teruel* by Juan Eugenio Hartzenbusch, staged at the Teatro del Príncipe on January 19, 1837; and *Don Juan Tenorio* by José Zorrilla, staged at the Teatro del Príncipe on March 28, 1844.

Looking at the dates on which each play made its debut, Allison Peers' bold assertion appears less extreme. Of the six plays named above, which critical consensus holds as the choicest of the Spanish Romantics' dramatic production, five belong to the initial years of the decade suggested and only one to the tenth year—there are none in between (1838-1843). The dismal situation of the theater becomes, thus, more and more glaring. It is against this seriously deficient background that Espronceda made his foray into the Spanish theater.

III. The Comedy *Ni el tío ni el sobrino*

On April 25, 1834 Espronceda's *Ni el tío ni el sobrino* was staged at the Teatro de la Cruz. Its premiere, thus, fell exactly between Martínez de la Rosa's *La conjuración de Venecia* and Larra's *Macías*. It was not only overshadowed by both of these works but also by Bretón de los Herreros' *Elena*, a play of dubious distinction by any standard, produced a few months later at the Teatro del Príncipe on October 23, 1834.

Ni el tío ni el sobrino, a three act play done in *romance octosílabo* is a comedy of manners' vaguely reminiscent of Leandro Fernández de Moratín's *El viejo y la niña* and *El sí de las niñas*, the latter of which it parodies according to Casalduero.' Written in collaboration with his friend Antonio Ros de Olano, it earned Espronceda no glory but neither did it discourage him from trying his hand at playwriting again, unquestionably improving his further attempt in quest for theatrical success.

This comedy is set in Madrid during a winter afternoon and evening, thus lasting only a few hours. Act I, divided into eight scenes, introduces all of the main characters except for one (Colonel Juan Renzuelo) who is believed to have died, and exposes the intrigue that will be further complicated in Act II before it is resolved and explained at the end of Act III.

In Act I Doña Paca tries to marry off her daughter Luisa to the rich and ridiculous old Don Martín. In order to gain an advantage Doña Paca claims to be the widow of Colonel Juan Renzuelo, supposedly killed by a bomb in Caracas, Venezuela. Don Martín, Renzuelo's best friend, believes her and gives both the feigned widow and her daughter food and shelter in his own home. With Martín live his nephew, Eugenio, and a manservant, Ambrosio. The former, secretly in love with Luisa, goes beserk upon discovering that his uncle Martín plans to marry the girl. Meanwhile, Don Carlos, a judicious friend of Martín, upon observing the proceedings, warns the old fool to beware of Paca and Luisa's intentions, that they may not be all above reproach. Hearing Don Carlos' advice, Martín, blinded by his vanity and arrogance, believes that his friend is also in love with Luisa and that the warnings given are really self-serving since Don Carlos wants the girl for himself.

The stage is set then for the development and complication of this conflict: two scheming women, Paca and Luisa, intent on taking advantage of a rich old fool, Martín. Eugenio's feeling for Luisa, though not totally exposed as of yet, can't help but further embroil the action. Ambrosio's role also remains unclear at this time, but customarily, given their intimate knowledge of their masters' lives, servants play significant parts in the course of the action.

By this time the characters' personalities are well enough delineated, though a few surprises await. Don Martín, the «Uncle» of the title, is portrayed as old though he pretends that he is young, as being rich though he is miserly with his money, as being pursued by many women though his only attraction is his wealth. So conceited is he that, at his ripe age (over sixty) and in spite of all of his shortcomings, he believes that Luisa loves only him and at that only for himself.

Doña Paca's character is not as rounded. She comes across as a calculating woman, solely intent on marrying her daughter into money. Given Paca's strong and dominating character we can guess that Luisa is merely an instrument for her. Once secure in the position of mother-in-law Paca would dominate over her young and weak daughter and her old and ridiculous son-in-law, taking control over money, house and servants for her own ends. The transparency of her lies to Martín, whom she praises to a level of absurdity, suggests her ineptness and stupidity—even though the fact that Martín believes everything Paca tells him underscores even further his own conceit and senility.

Luisa, a pawn in her mother's battle of wits with Martín, seems to have no will of her own and is content to appear pretty and overtly attracted to Martín (though secretly she despises him) as Paca instructs her, either through parroting recitals of her virtuousness or her feigned tender love for the old man. Nonetheless, Luisa does not seem so despicable a character as her mother Paca or as dislikeable as Martín.

Eugenio is portrayed by the dramatists as a bumbling idiot, stumbling over tables and chairs, breaking china cups, never finishing his sentences and repeating himself constantly. The most cardboard-like figure in the whole play, Eugenio is neither agreeable nor hateful, but simply unbelievable as a character. His role as a younger, more attractive, secret rival to his uncle for Luisa's love is totally unexploited due to a characterization that lacks verisimulitude in every regard.

Don Carlos, in his role as a good friend of Martín and an outsider who has some objectivity and a better perspective on things, is quite credible. His speech, his reasonings, his approach to the conflict and his attitude in general make him the most reliable of all of the personnages encountered so far. Don Carlos not only sees through Paca's pretensions but also is aware of Martín's presumptuousness and how he should be handled in order to bring about the desired results—uncover the woman's ploy but without unduly hurting Martín's overly-high regard of himself.

As the first of the ten scenes of Act II opens, Martín's manservant

Ambrosio walks in on Paca and Luisa, who continue to plot, and discovers their plan to gain control of his employer's wealth through matrimony. Ambrosio, pretending unswerving fidelity to Martín, appears indignant at the two women though Paca encounters few obstacles in persuading him to join them, promising to turn over to him half of Luisa's dowry. Just at the moment when Ambrosio has decided to accept and subsequently demand some sort of security so that Paca would not dismiss him outright after the supposed marriage, in walks Don Carlos who doubtless has heard enough to convince him that his worst suspicions were well-founded. Paca, Ambrosio and Luisa change the topic but Don Carlos begins, with mordant irony, to taunt Luisa and her mother about their honesty and their character as Ambrosio leaves, supposedly to carry a message to Martín. Just as unexpectedly as Don Carlos had appeared moments before, Martín now enters the room where his friend is trying to get the ladies to admit to their scheme. The old man, however, misinterprets once again Don Carlos' attempt to protect him from the two gold diggers. A quarrel between the men ensues, Martín insults Don Carlos and the latter issues a challenge to a duel in order to cleanse his name and his honor. It is after Don Carlos' departure that we discover a new trait of Martín's—cowardice. Much as he tries to weasel out of the duel, the fawning women cannot offer Martín a way out in spite of the fact that he now blames them—instead of his quick tongue—for his predicament. Later in his own quarters, when Martín shakenly answers the door expecting to see Don Carlos' second, a man attired in military uniform addresses him as an old friend absent for many years. Martín can hardly believe his eyes when he recognizes none other than Juan Renzuelo whom he'd considered dead for quite some time. Martín now faces another dilemma: Renzuelo can probably help him find a way out of the duel, but what about his own plan to marry Luisa, the Colonel's daughter? Won't Renzuelo feel that he, Martín, has been taking unfair advantage of the destitute girl and her mother while ostensibly offering them a roof over their heads? Contrary to Martín's expectations, his friend the Colonel, mindful of military honor, not only does not offer to help in the confrontation with Don Carlos but goes so far as to drag the cowardly Martín to his antagonist's house. As to how Renzuelo will react to Martín's pretended matrimony with Luisa, is not revealed until the final act.

In this second act two new characters are encountered for the first time: Ambrosio and Juan Renzuelo. Ambrosio turns out to be a scoundrel willing to sell himself to the highest bidder. He trades loyalty for lucre without any compunction and makes matters worse for himself not only in front of the audience, to whom he is no longer sympathetic once he allies himself with Paca and Luisa, but with the two women as well when he demands a guarantee to secure his position in the future—meaning that he doubts Paca's promise of his reward of half of Luisa's dowry once the mother assumes command of the household. Colonel Juan Renzuelo's surprising appearance toward the end of Act II both complicates the action and at the same time begins to tie loose ends. His presence means that Paca and Luisa's cover has been undone. Only by his being dead and remaining absent could the charade have succeeded. Now that he is very alive and in no way related to them, their hand has been lost. The Colonel's demeanor as a straightforward, sincere and intimate friend is perhaps the most engaging and believable of the entire work. Like Don Carlos he too functions well as a credible personnage.

The thirteen brief scenes of Act III contain the moralizing dénouement of the play. Martín and Renzuelo appear in Don Carlos' house where the two antagonists reconcile after Martín, feigning ill health too severe for duelling, admits his mistake and vaguely apologizes. Having done away with his most serious peril, Martín then decides to tackle the problem of the wedding only to find that Renzuelo, convinced that he has neither a wife nor a daughter, does not object in the least to the marriage. Meanwhile back at Paca's, Ambrosio has been telling the two woman of Renzuelo's reappearance. Luisa, feeling that all has been lost, is ready to give up the gambit, but not so her mother. Paca convinces the daughter to instead flee with Eugenio, the «Nephew» of the play's title and of Martín whom he should soon inherit, since Paca is confident that in the impending duel Martín is sure to die. Luisa has no trouble convincing the gullible Eugenio—who is secretly in love with her—that her seeming love for his uncle was forced upon her and that they should run away together because it is he, Eugenio, whom she has really cared for all along. The desperate gamble fails, however, because with the arrival of Don Carlos, Ambrosio, and especially Colonel Renzuelo and Martín to confront Paca and Luisa, the entire plot is uncovered. The women go away shamefacedly, Ambrosio is fired, Eugenio is left without a lover, and Martín loses the jewels and other presents he had given to Luisa and her mother.

The last two verses of the play, «Viejo que casa con niña, / o lleva víctima, o maula,» pretty well crystallize the reason for its commercial and critical failure. There is nothing new or romantic about a comedy of errors or manners where mistaken identities are foiled as good triumphs over evil and everyone gets his or her just desserts in a colloquial and mildly moralizing manner. Francisco Martínez de la Rosa's *La conjuración de Venecia*, the stage's first political historical drama, had premiered only two days before and the way was paved for a new sort of dramatic bent, whether it be the melancholy sentiment of unlucky lovers such as Larra's medieval troubador *Macías* staged later that year, or the violent and impassioned romanticism of *Don Alvaro* that was to come less than one year after Espronceda's and Ros de Olano's *Ni el tío ni el sobrino*. All in all, nevertheless, this comedy is not totally without redemption. Larra in his review of the play for the Madrid journal *La Revista Española* perhaps summed up best the limited laudable qualities of *Ni el tío ni el sobrino*: «El diálogo nos ha parecido fluido y correcto; no carece de chistes, de viveza y naturalidad, y es buena su versificación.»[10]

IV. The Drama *Amor venga sus agravios*

Espronceda had tried, with his friend Antonio Ros de Olano, to have their play *Ni el tío ni el sobrino* staged at the prestigious Teatro del Príncipe, but without success; they had to settle for the Teatro de la Cruz. Four years later when *Amor venga sus agravios* opened, it was finally at the Teatro del Príncipe as Espronceda and his new collaborator, Eugenio Moreno López, had wished. Perhaps the betterment of locale can be ascribed not merely to Espronceda's growing fame but also to a vastly superior play. Certainly the reviews and theatrical notices which appeared following the September 23, 1838 premiere are appreciably more favorable than those pertaining to *Ni el tío ni el sobrino*.[11]

Only three completely original plays were produced in 1838,[12] among them Espronceda's, advertised under the authorship of Luis Senra y Palomares, the pseudonym chosen by the poet and his collaborator Moreno López. The diminishing number of theater works suggests that by this date the best of the romantic dramas had been already produced, save for Zorrilla's *Don Juan Tenorio*. The last of these had been seen one year before on January 19, 1837—Hartzenbusch's *Los amantes de Teruel*. Espronceda, thus, had very little choice but to write his play in a more original or at least current fashion if he hoped for any kind of success. He may or may not have been aware of it but time was running out for romantic drama.

Amor venga sus agravios, written in prose and divided into five acts, is a historical drama of tragic dimensions, situated in the years 1623-1624 during the reign of the young Hapsburg King Felipe IV. Inevitable are the parallels and ascendancies that this latest play of Espronceda's shares with either Golden Age dramas, such as Guillén de Castro's *Las mocedades del Cid* or else with works of other Romantics such as the Duke of Rivas' historical ballad «El Cuento de un veterano» published in 1837.[13] However,

Amor venga sus agravios can be read or viewed without one's being constantly reminded of its possible antecedents such is the power of its plot, the passions that move its protagonists and the inexorability of its ending. These foregoing considerations render it closer to a classic than to a romantic drama: the characters are flawed internally as human beings by blinding passions that carry them to their ultimate destruction. Alvaro de Mendoza, a forerunner of the satanic hero of *El estudiante de Salamanca,* Don Félix de Montemar, is driven by a thirst for power and wealth. Clara, the object of his attentions but in love with someone else, thinks of nothing but murder with which to avenge the death of her lover, Pedro Figueroa. The latter moves impelled by jealousy that makes him fear for the loss of Clara to the arrogant and martial Mendoza. In the end all three die by Clara's hand in a conclusion not too dissimilar from Rivas' *Don Alvaro o la fuerza del sino,* [14] with the important difference that the romantic heroine, here no longer pure but instead insane albeit still passionate, causes the demise of those she hates and those she loves as well as her own.

Amor venga sus agravios does not rely on devices such as coincidences, byzantine recognitions (anagnorisis) or the easy and disappointing tricks observed in *Ni el tío ni el sobrino* to unfold its disastrous plot. Instead the audience is thrust into a classic triangle of love, hate, jealousy and greed where two men and a woman are inextricably caught.

The drama begins just prior to an event that will alter the lives of all of the main characters. All three are introduced in Act I and almost at once the factor that will bring about their end can be fully understood. On a May morning in the year 1623, Alvaro de Mendoza, a famous army captain recently arrived from the war in Flanders, strolls among the gardens of Madrid's Retiro Park where he meets his old friend, Pacheco, and explains that the reason for his unexpected return is his impending marriage to his cousin, the rich Clara, Marquisa of Palma, whom he does not know very well. Soon Clara's guardian, the Count of Piedrahíta, who has arranged the wedding, and then Clara herself appear on the scene. Though less interested in being awarded her love than her title and fortune as her future consort, Mendoza cannot help but notice that Clara's attention is directed towards Pedro Figueroa who has been observing from afar the intimate circle made up by the two supposed lovers, her uncle, a priest and Pacheco. Also noticed by Mendoza is a letter given by one of Clara's servants to Figueroa. Imagining that the note contains an invitation to a date, Mendoza, mindful of his pride and his honor, circles the surroundings of the girl's mansion later that evening and indeed foils an attempt by Clara and Figueroa to visit together.

By the end of Act I Mendoza is revealed as a penniless but proud and famous soldier who counts himself lucky to have such bright marriage prospects: a young, beautiful, noble and wealthy bride. He has the approval of her tutor and of the court of the King. Clara, a not so pure and ingenuous young woman, knows her own mind and intends to marry one of her own vassals, Figueroa—not Mendoza—no matter what the cost. Figueroa appears as the man in love and in turn loved, but very much aware that his hold on Clara is neither known nor supported by any higher powers, and thus is afraid and insanely jealous that she will not be his. Mendoza would seem to have the upper hand here except for Clara's determination and her love for Figueroa and the latter's total devotion to her.

Act II takes place in its entirety in Clara's rooms. As she ponders the previous nights' fiasco where a disguised Mendoza had impeded Figueroa's meeting with her and darkened their prospects for a future together, the Count of Piedrahíta and Father Rafael come in to make arrangements for Clara's wedding to Mendoza. Angered at his charges' refusal to accept his wishes, the tutor threatens Clara and leaves, whereupon she addresses another note to Figueroa calling for his help. Mendoza, however, on his way to see Clara, intercepts the message and a violent confrontation ensues between the two of them. The arrival of Figueroa, awaited by Mendoza, ends this second act, and as the curtain falls the two rivals walk away toward a duel where Figueroa is left for dead by the captain.

The meeting between Mendoza and Figueroa having taken place offstage, Act III begins with a scene that reflects Spain's bureaucracy at work, her dubious foreign policy and the palace intrigues of the early 1600s. Mendoza, his protector the Count of Piedrahíta, and a chosen few courtiers banter with King Felipe IV when a mourning Clara enters the royal chamber demanding justice for her slain lover, due her station as a titled noblewoman, and points an accusing finger at Mendoza. In the emotion and haste of the moment the King orders the guilty one taken prisoner, a command soon rescinded and transferred to Clara who is ordered to spend the rest of her days in a convent or consent to marrying Mendoza. The turn of events is so calamitous for Clara that when confronted by this choice, announced to her by Mendoza himself, the girl begins a metamorphosis into madness (scene iv) slowly paving the way for her final actions at the end of Act V. She can not bear to have lost her lover, her fortune and her freedom to Mendoza who is now entitled to do as he pleases having inherited, by reason of their relationship, all that she forfeits by entering the cloister.

Act IV opens with another general prelude that portrays the grand lifestyle now enjoyed by the opportunist Mendoza, a scene further amplified at the beginning of Act V when a bacchanalian feast drags on for most of July 11, 1624, the last day of his life. A year and a half has passed since last he was seen, when Figueroa, forgotten and indeed thought dead by everyone, appears in Mendoza's house demanding satisfaction once more; but Mendoza, in perfect self-control, refuses another duel and the often defeated rival, humbled yet again, withdraws avowing revenge for himself and for Clara. She, aware of his being alive, beckons Figueroa to her cell, where interrupted in their love colloquium, he must hide in an ark as she faints, overcome by the fear of the discovery of their tryst.

Act V resembles, more than any other, Espronceda's later *El Estudiante de Salamanca* in many respects. Don Alvaro de Mendoza, leading a dissipated life of womanizing, drinking and idleness is seen dining with a group of friends at his mansion on a summer evening. As the wine and the songs flow freely, Mendoza receives a warning to change his ways from Father Rafael who is jeered by all those present, vinous to the last. Following his departure, a perfumed letter enticing Mendoza to a midnight rendevous is delivered and read aloud by him, an invitation he hurries to accept so eagerly that at eleven-thirty he leaves his guests behind awaiting his return and the recounting of his adventure. The author of the note is none other than Clara whose insanity, further augmented by the discovery of Figueroa's cadaver in her ark where he asphyxiated, plans not a love encounter but rather a murder. After a dialogue filled with Mendoza's flirtatious bonhomie and Clara's double entendres, she succeeds in bringing death to the object of her hatred—having shown him Figueroa's body—and to herself as they both drink from a poisoned glass. Lacking both a love and a hate object to consume her, she has no further use for life.

In terms of the romantic aesthetic, the drama succeeds on many counts: passions rule, love brings misfortune on those who seek it, conflicts are personalized, the conclusion is predictably calamitous and the characters embody in their respective male and female roles the expected traits of *donjuanismo* and alternatively passion-purity and madness. In *Amor venga sus agravios* Espronceda and Moreno López have gone beyond stereotyped romantic theatre, making the characters, the emotions and the situations credible and empathetic. Furthermore Pacheco's lines,

> ¿Sabeis que es un asunto excelente para una comedia? Una marquesa enamorada de un vasallo suyo, un primo que vuelve de Flandes, un desafío con el amante, de cuyas resultas la triste señora entró monja. ¡Vota va!, que es lástima que nuestro don Pedro Calderón no la tome por su cuenta. (Act IV, scene i)

show more than a passing awareness on the part of the dramatists that self-parody perhaps should not be too far removed. Espronceda, at least, was very conscious of the art of making literature and his latest play exemplifies such an undertaking. Life can serve Art well, even if the character Pacheco says it tongue in cheek.

V. The Tragedy *Blanca de Borbón*

Not only did the Romantics have a real interest in historical periods of Spain's centuries past, but quite a few of them seem to have focused on certain figures with special fixation. One of these was Pedro I el Cruel, King of Castille in the years 1351-1369, a figure that had also held some fascination for several Golden Age playwrights among them Lope de Vega, Tirso de Molina and Calderón de la Barca as witnessed in their respective dramas *El Infanzón de Illescas, El Rey Don Pedro en Madrid* and *El médico de su honra.* Closer to Espronceda's time, in the first half of the nineteenth century, we find no less than seven other works dealing with either the mid-fourteenth century reign of Pedro I, the person of the King, or else with the misfortunes befallen his wife Blanca. Dionino Solis (né Dionisio Villanueva y Ochoa) titled his play *Blanca de Borbón*, as did Antonio Gil y Zárate, the same as Espronceda's; José María Iñiguez called his *Doña Blanca,* while Manuel José Quintana's work, now lost to us, was titled *Doña Blanca de Borbón;* and finally José Zorrilla penned no less than three dramas about Pedro I el Cruel, *El zapatero y el rey,* parts I and II, and *El Molino de Guadalajara.*

It is difficult at this point to say what it was exactly about Pedro I el Cruel that drew the attention of the Romantics, but a good supposition would be that the personage's high station (a crowned king), the period of his reign (medieval times), his notoriously evil character (cruel, despotic and tempestuous), his marital affairs (execution of his wife) and his violent death (killed by his half-brother Enrique de Trastamara) provided them with plenty of raw material to construct their own fantastic or legendary version of history that would not be too far-fetched from reality. And while some viewed Pedro I as a bold, larger-than-life character whose adventures exhibited greatness and bravery among other virtues, Espronceda chose instead to portray him as a despot under whom freedom disappeared, subservience was substituted for loyalty and resistance became the sole means of maintaining one's honor.

The exact circumstances of the composition of Espronceda's most critically successful play are somewhat obscure, most of all the date(s) of its writing since, as noted earlier, not until 1870—twenty-eight years after the author's death—was it published and then in an extremely limited edition done by his daughter Blanca and her brother-in-law, Patricio de la Escosura, who had been a close friend of the poet. Not until 1907 did the British scholar Philip H. Churchman publish a critical annotated edition of the play in the journal *Revue Hispanique* (volume 17, pages 549-777). Unfortunately Mr. Churchman did not try to sort out the chronology of the work; consequently, most scholars—confronted with an undated play which has never been put on the stage—are left with two alternatives to ascertain its dating. One is to do it through the intrinsic merits of the work, its themes, character development, versification and other similar analyses so as to place it at some point in the author's stage of development. A second possibility is to try to establish its age through an extrinsic approach by means of such scholarly sleuthing as determining the brand and age of the paper's watermark, ownership of an extant manuscript, etc. Because there are three manuscripts[15] of *Blanca de Borbón* and also because it is the only play Espronceda authored alone—and therefore difficult to compare with the other two dramas done in collaboration—the theories resulting from the first suggested method yield conflicting dates and modes of composition. Patricio de la Escosura suggests the dates 1834 to 1836 and advances the theory that the first two acts were done long before the remaining three, a theory largely accepted by Bonilla y San Martín, Blanca de Espronceda and Churchman.[16] José Cascales Muñoz, basing his arguments also on intrinsic considerations, gives as a plausible date the year 1838.[17] However, it was not until the publication of R. Marrast's literary detective work in 1971 that *Blanca de Borbón* could be dated with complete certainty as having been written somewhat earlier, between 1831 and 1832.[18] The means employed by Professor Marrast were the collection of the three editions known to exist both through the changes made in each as well as through the age of manufacture of the sheets of paper on which they are written.

In spite of it all, the disparity of the conjectured and the actual dates of the composition does not cause undue disbelief or surprise because, though now we know that *Blanca de Borbón* antedates *Ni el tío ni el sobrino* and *Amor venga sus agravios*, the earlier play is in all respects superior to the other two and seemingly the work of a more mature author, perhaps suggesting that the collaborators' contributions were not too efficacious. It is a pity that it was not staged despite the support of Juan Grimaldi, the director of the Teatro del Príncipe, as well as the company of actors of this theater, due to censorship problems that caused Espronceda to file away the revised manuscript and not think about it again. Judging from its late-surfacing critical success, it might have assured its author the commercial and public acclaim he sought in vain with his other two plays.

Written in five acts and in *romance heroico,* a verse form vaguely reminiscent of the traditional neo-classical plays, *Blanca de Borbón* relates the tragic life endured by Pedro I el Cruel's wife, the efforts by the King's vassals to overthrow him and the oppressiveness of a court governed by intrigue and self-aggrandizement. The tone, the passions involved, the settings, the actions and the personages all characterize this play as a romantic tragedy in spite of the unexpected observance of the three dramatic unities of space, time and action by Espronceda.

Act I (nine scenes) takes place in the fortress where Blanca is held prisoner by order of King Pedro, her husband. This theme, familiar to the Espronceda reader, is given life throughout the play. Blanca suffers captive, while outside the birth of a bastard son to the King by his concubine María de Padilla is being celebrated. Much like the unfortunate prisoner awaiting death in the poem «Reo de muerte» (see Chapter Four), Blanca's grief at being incarcerated without justifiable cause is exacerbated by the vituperation and mockery that an adultress usurping her place as a wife and a Queen has perpetrated. Here, and continuing throughout the whole play, we are struck by Blanca's total lack of guile, her unwavering devotion to a husband who is cruel and responsible for her imprisonment, her concern for the man who truly loves her (Enrique de Trastamara, the King's half-brother) while remaining faithful to Pedro, the composure with which she maintains a royal dignity in the face of her jailers (Tello and his soldiers) and of those seeking to destroy her (García de Padilla, the King's counselor and brother of the concubine), and the acceptance with which she acknowledges the approaching end of her life.

Nearly the whole act consists of a series of scenes that either directly, through her presence, or indirectly, by exchanges between the other characters, show Blanca's long suffering and her innocence of all blame while, in counter-point fashion, revealing the scheming heartlessness of the King's inner circle for whom Blanca's death becomes necessary in order to insure their continued prosperity, especially that of García and his sister la Padilla.

Act II (10 scenes) shifts location to the King's palace, the Alcázar of Sevilla, offering a marked contrast with its airy salons and garden in the background to the iron bars and sparse furnishings where Blanca is forced to dwell. Pedro I el Cruel is seen here for the first time, coming across as a forceful, capricious despot perhaps not entirely evil but surrounded by traitors who influence him against the good of the kingdom and especially against his wife Blanca. The King wavers between the ill-intended, self-serving advice he hears and his own more noble inclinations and thus the audience does not feel complete antipathy toward him. He is, however, flawed because he listens to the flattery and the sycophantic council given him by his concubine and her brother.

Toward the end of this second act the threat of armed revolt against the King becomes more real, fueled by his half-brother Enrique de Trastamara—pretender to the throne and Blanca's would-be lover liberator—and Fernando de Castro whose sister, Juana, had been earlier forsaken by Pedro in the role of another wife. Aiding these two figures, whose motive for their antagonism to the King would appear to be revenge of a very personal sort, are courtiers such as the elder Hernando interested in the welfare of the kingdom and seeking an end to Pedro's reliance on his corrupt favorites.

Act III (7 scenes) takes place at night out in the open field where on the right Blanca's prison can be seen and where on the left of the stage the cave dwelling of a witch and her son Abenfarax is located. The course of the action follows expected paths: la Padilla conspires with the Witch to ensure Blanca's ill-fate, Enrique meets again with his beloved and promises to free her, and Pedro and Enrique finally meet face to face. In this encounter a sword fight is averted when Enrique realizes that he cannot draw his against a brother and the King supposes that to exile Enrique would be a worse punishment than death—an error in judgement for which Pedro would pay with his life as the witch predicts at the end of this third act: «¡La vida sí, te arrancará tu hermano!». In historical fact, at the castle of Montiel, Enrique de Trastamara killed his half-brother Pedro I el Cruel with a dagger in the year 1369 and thus ascended to the throne.

The most striking note of Act III however is the figure of Abenfarax, son of the witch. At the opening of the first scene Abenfarax sharpens his knife and, showing it to his mother, rejoices at the thought of the blood it will draw to appease the infernal spirits of their cave and slake his own thirst for murder and death. His characterization as evil incarnate makes him a precursor of one of Spanish literature's most inimitable characters in the twentieth century: Valle Inclán's crazed Fuso Negro in *Romance de lobos* and *Cara de Plata,* two of this author's best plays. Abenfarax is a monomaniacal monster—«esperpento» as Valle later called it—who thinks of blood, knives and killings to the exclusion of everything else, truly a dark humanoid whose mother, an infernal figure herself though more conventional in her cunning vileness, was impregnated by demons.[19]

In Act IV (9 scenes) Pedro and Blanca meet for the first and only time in an emotionally charged fourth scene, an encounter that the hateful concubine la Padilla fails to prevent, fearful though she is that Blanca's innocence would suffice to convince the King of his mistaken ways. The meeting takes place in the throne room where la Padilla sits next to the King and Blanca kneels humbled at their feet. Blanca's plea for a return to their marital state and for forgiveness, although patently sincere and tearful, goes unattended by Pedro who nevertheless is almost moved to end her life by his own hand as she begs him to do. In the following scene, Pedro doubts the justice of his decree, grieved by Blanca's unabashed emotional appeal and her declaration of love, but once again his concubine's poisoned rationalizations erase his concerns for the wronged wife. Already a victim of fate, Blanca is further damned when an ill-timed and unsuccessful revolt is quashed by Pedro in his castle and García and Padilla accuse her and Enrique of fomenting the rebellion. Enraged by what he believes to be indeed a conspiracy, Pedro disowns Blanca whose life is placed in the hands of García, a man only too eager to have her put to death when his sister la Padilla enjoins him to do so. The unjust execution, opposed even by her unsympathetic jailer, Tello, is to be carried out by the bloodthirsty Abenfarax.

Aware that her death is fast approaching, Blanca at the end of the scene seven utters those words heard so often in Espronceda's writings: «Sólo en la paz de la callada tumba/ puede esperar a su dolor remedio.» «A Jarifa en una orgía,» *El Estudiante de Salamanca* and *El Diablo Mundo* all express a similar notion in which Espronceda must have believed sincerely enough to account for its constant reiteration.

Act V (7 scenes), the shortest one of all, returns to the location of the third act: an exterior with the witch's cave on the left and Blanca's fortress-prison on the right of the stage. Storms rage in the night as Blanca prepares herself for death when a hooded hermit comes to console her. The hermit turns out to be none other than Enrique who offers Blanca a final chance to escape—the revolt having been unsuccessful—in his disguise. She refuses, fearing for her life, whereupon Enrique and his men take the castle by force but as he is about to come into her chamber to set her free, the satanic Abenfarax slits her throat, killing her instantly. The assassin then falls under Enrique's sword. Enrique, unable to do anything more for the woman he has loved, swears on a crucifix not to return his sword to its sheath until all those responsible for Blanca's death are made to pay for their misdeed.

So ends *Blanca de Borbón*, a tragedy written in the best neoclassic form but infused with undeniably romantic characters, motives, themes, plots and subplots and a tableau that does not totally eschew Espronceda's most cherished ideal: freedom for all in all respects. The death of Blanca de

Borbón (sister-in-law of Charles V of France and only twenty-five years old when she was put to death) even manages to illustrate once more the poet's deep-seated, pessimistic conviction that life cannot bear anything but the most bitter fruit to those beings endowed with sensibility for higher ideals and to whom the peace of the sepulchre appears as the sole certainty of their existence.

NOTES

1. Gustavo Adolfo Bécquer, like Espronceda, also wrote plays in collaboration with others under the pseudonyms of Adolfo García and Adolfo Rodríguez. His best known plays are: *La novia y el pantalón,* 1856; *La venta encantada,* 1859; *Las distracciones*, 1859; *Tal para cual,* 1860; *La cruz del valle,* 1860; *El nuevo Fígaro*, 1862; and *Clara de Rosemberg,* 1863. See Juan Antonio Tamayo, *Teatro de Gustavo Adolfo Bécquer* (Madrid: Consejo Superior de Investigaciones Científicas, 1949).

2. *Blanca de Borbón. Drama Trájico [sic] en Cinco Actos y en Verso. Obra Inédita de Espronceda*. Pública su hija Blanca. Madrid: Impresa por las nietas del autor Luz y Laura, 1870, 117 pp.

3. Ricardo Navas Ruiz, *El Romanticismo Español* (Salamanca: Anaya, 1970), p. 81.

4. Edgar Allison Peers, *Historia de movimiento romántico español*, Vol. II (Madrid: Gredos, 1954), p. 16.

5. Navas Ruiz, *op. cit.,* p. 77.

6. Quoted from Fernando Fernández de Córdoba, *Mis memorias íntimas* (Madrid: Rivadeneyra, 1886-1889), by Navas Ruiz, *op. cit.,* pp. 78-79.

7. Navas Ruiz, p. 78.

8. Robert Marrast, *José de Espronceda: El estudiante de Salamanca. El diablo mundo* (Madrid: Castalia, 1978), pp. 347-48.

9. Joaquín Casalduero, *Espronceda* (Madrid, 1967), p. 260.

10. Mariano José Larra (Fígaro), «Primera representación de *Ni el tío ni el sobrino.*» *BAE,* vol. 127 (Madrid, 1960), p. 388.

11. See especially Enrique Gil y Carrasco's review in *El correo nacional* of October 4, 1838.

12. Allison Peers, *op. cit.,* Vol. II, pp. 249-50.

13. Daniel G. Samuels, «Some Spanish Romantic Debts of Espronceda,» *Hispanic Review,* 16 (1948), 158-60.

14. *Ibid.,* p. 160.

15. Two are deposited in the British Museum and one in the Biblioteca Menéndez y

Pelayo in Santander (Spain). For other pertinent data consult Robert Marrast's fascinating article «Contribution a la Bibliographie d'Espronceda: Les manuscrits et la date de *Blanca de Borbón*,» *Bulletin Hispanique*, 73 (1971), 125-32.

16.   See Churchman's preface to *Blanca de Borbón*, op. cit., pp. 549-560.

17.   José Cascales Muñoz, *Espronceda: Su época, su vida y sus obras* (Madrid: Biblioteca Hispana, 1914), pp. 113-15.

18.   See footnote 15 above.

19.   In Act V, scene vi, Abenfarax says: «Una bruja / y un hijo de Luzbel fueron mis padres.»

CHAPTER EIGHT

The Prose Writings

Even if Espronceda's prose were not put up against his verse works, a comparison most critics are fond of making, it would hardly be considered of anthology quality. And yet Espronceda's prose writings make worthwhile reading for several reasons. They are among his first published pieces and prefigure many of the preoccupations which will later be fully and more artistically revealed in the verse works. With the freer, open-ended format of the essays comes a less stylized portrait of the times in which Espronceda wrote. And lastly both the fiction and the non-fiction prose works contain physical and spiritual autobiographical accounts found nowhere else in Espronceda's production.

I. The Historical Novel and its Presence in Spain

The historical novel in Spain never reached great heights either critically or commercially, at least in its indigenous form. The publication of translations and imitations abounded, of course, because they constituted the only means of achieving some success with any degree of certainty. Sir Walter Scott, Alessandro Manzoni, Victor Hugo and Alexander Dumas outsold their Spanish counterparts many times over. Scott's *Ivanhoe*, for example, published in 1819, had undergone at least five translations from English to Spanish by the time Espronceda's novel *Sancho Saldaña o El Castellano de Cuéllar. Novela histórica original del siglo XIII* appeared in 1834.[1]

The influence exerted by Walter Scott's fiction is all-pervasive in the Spanish historical novel as well as in other national literatures. It was Scott, after all, who invented the genre with the so-called *Waverly* series of novels begun in 1814 with a novel of this title. These narrative fiction works, set in medieval times with plots of adventure and intrigue, had as their backdrops recognizable historical and geographical settings. Their success and, thus, their influence were immediate and lasting as the titles *Rob Roy, Quentin Durward, The Talisman, Kenilworth* and the already cited *Ivanhoe*, among many critics, can attest. Discounting Telesforo Trueba y Cossios' 1829 novel *The Castilian,* dealing (again) with Pedro I el Cruel and Enrique de Trastamara's fratricidal wars, a narrative written in English during Trueba's exile in England and not seen in a Spanish version until 1845, Scott's imprint, above all in *Ivanhoe*, can be unerringly recognized time and time again in the novels of the few Romantics in Spain that cultivated this genre. Among these, Ramón López Soler was the most prolific and popular but typically not very original. His first novel *Los bandos de Castilla,* issued in 1830, a work that by common consent inaugurates the historical novel in Spain, is nothing more than an unabashed adaptation of *Ivanhoe.* Soler's other bestseller, *La catedral de Sevilla,* follows faithfully the pattern set by Victor Hugo's *Notre Dame de Paris.* In truth, adhering to a more or less strict critical criterion, only two historical novels written in Spanish might qualify as both original and artistically meritorious. They are Mariano José de Larra's *El doncel de don Enrique el Doliente,* on the subject of the medieval troubador who also protagonized his drama *Macías*, and Enrique Gil y Carrasco's *El Señor de Bembibre,* published a decade after Larra's novel in 1844.

II. History and Story:
Sancho Saldaña o El Castellano de Cuéllar

Following the Regent Queen María Cristina's proclamation of amnesty for political prisoners and exiles issued on October 15, 1832, Espronceda began plotting his return to Spain from France after a long five years in exile that had begun in the month of August of 1827. He crossed the Franco-Spanish border at the Pyrenees in the first days of March, 1833, followed almost immediately by Teresa Mancha. Back in Madrid, Espronceda went to live with his mother at number 3 San Miguel Street while Teresa was provided with an apartment near the poet's residence at number 1 on the same street. He soon fell back into his routine of friends, cafe gatherings, literary occupations and political intrigues while Teresa languished alone, seemingly more and more forgotten in a relationship that became progressively less important to Espronceda. Accepted into the Corps of Royal Guards, he appears to have committed the unforgiveable blunder of reading, one night at a well-attended banquet, a string of verses censorious of the ailing King that some present considered subversive enough not only to have Espronceda expelled from the Corps but also to see him exiled once again from the court city of Madrid for an unspecified number of months. Since, thankfully, all that was demanded of the culprit, aside from his dismissal from the Guard, was that he leave the capital, Espronceda chose to go to the small town of Cuéllar in the nearby province of Segovia. The reason for this choice had much to do with the fact that the lord mayor of the town was none other than Miguel Ortiz y Amor, one of the founding members of the secret society of their adolescent years, «Los Numantinos,» which had earlier resulted in a similar sentence of exile for the conspirators served by Espronceda in Guadalajara in 1825. Whereas during that previous stay Espronceda had worked on the long epic poem «El Pelayo,» this time in the summer months of 1833, the poet wrote much of his one and only novel, dedicated to his mother María del Carmen, *Sancho Saldaña o El Castellano de Cuéllar. Novela histórica original del siglo XIII* as the title reads. By the time of his return to Madrid soon after the death of Fernando VII on September 24, 1833, most of the work must have been near completion, at least in a first-draft format, since on January 2 of the following year the first two volumes of a projected six were submitted to the official government censorship board. And on February 5, Espronceda signed a contract with the Madrid publisher and bookseller, his friend, Manuel Delgado for six thousand *reales*—a considerable sum—whereby he, in turn, agreed to furnish a completed manuscript by the 31st of March. The first volume was offered for sale on April 8, 1834 and the sixth one on November 3 of the same year.[2] In all the novel consists of these six volumes divided into forty-eight chapters plus a conclusion in a total of 1,150 octavo pages. It is a work, then, of considerable length as it stood in 1834 but by no means is it as unmanageably extensive (1,794 pp.) as the 1869 edition would suggest. This latter version incorporates a second part that could not have been written by Espronceda. He had died some twenty-seven years earlier and, aside from that unassailable fact, the new characters that appear out of nowhere, the general spirit of the addition and the non-sequitur situations encountered have little in common with the original narrative design.

Four historical novels published in 1834 made it a banner year for the genre.[3] They were Estanislao de Cosca Vayo's *Los expatriados,* Larra's *El doncel de Don Enrique el Doliente,* López Soler's *La catedral de Sevilla* and Espronceda's own *Sancho Saldaña.*

Sancho Saldaña like most historical novels is constructed upon a historical skeleton, somewhat faithful to the people and events of a given period, and then fleshed out by the novelist with a plot protagonized by semi-legendary or fictitious characters where rivalries or love interests play a very significant role. Espronceda's novel has as its historical setting the last days of Alfonso X el Sabio and the reign of his son Sancho IV el Bravo spanning the years 1284-1295. Solidly documented,[4] *Sancho Saldaña* is based on the *Crónica del rey don Alfonso X*, the *Crónica de Sancho el Bravo* and the Jesuit Juan de Mariana's *Historiae de rebus Hispaniae*. As the rule of Sancho IV fell upon particularly turbulent times—intercine wars between Alfonso and Sancho, the death of Alfonso's eldest son D. Fernando de La Cerda and then his own demise, unending quarrels of the newly crowned monarch Sancho with the members of the La Cerda family branch and their partisans among the nobility, and continual political maneuverings between the Castilian and the Aragonese vassals—Espronceda had plenty of grist for his mill. Upon this he built *Sancho Saldaña*'s other half which in turn was modelled to a great degree upon Walter Scott's *Ivanhoe*.[5]

The similarities of characters and situations between the Scottsman's novel and the Spaniard's are irrefutable. Entire passages which may suggest perhaps reminiscences rather are plagiarism have been pointed out by Allison Peers in his lengthy essays on the subject.[6] Personnages, both invented and historical, in Espronceda's work hark back to Scott's on an almost one-to-one basis: the bandit El Velludo—Robin of Locksley and his Merry Men, King Sancho—King Richard, Hermano Zacarías—Friar Tuck, the dog Sagaz—the dog Fangs, Sancho Saldaña—Brian de Bois Guilbert, Hernando de Iscar—Wilfred of Ivanhoe, the Jew Abraham—the Jew Issac of York, Esther (Zoraida)—Rebecca.[7] Other similarities have been found to exist between *Sancho Saldaña* and *Quentin Durward, The Bride of Lamermoor, The Fair Maid of Perth* and *The Constable of Chester*.[8]

Without altogether dismissing Allison Peers contentions that *Sancho Saldaña* owes a great deal to some of Scott's *Waverly* novels, that it is not «anything more than a very mediocre novel»[9] or that it is «rather undistinguished,»[10] Nicholson B. Adams refutes that Espronceda's borrowings go beyond certain details and external parallels such as medieval customs, modes of dress, manners of speech and comportment. Whereas Scott's *Ivanhoe* is a work of optimism and triumph where characters thrive in perilous adventures, Espronceda's «whole novel is one of failure.»[11] In *Sancho Saldaña*, Leonor, Elvira and Zoraida, the three main feminine figures die, Sancho Saldaña becomes a Trappist monk, his antagonist, Hernando de Iscar flees the kingdom, and only one character, Usdróbal meets with any fortune, as he is knighted by the King Sancho.

In his perceptive contrapuntal essay to Allison Peer's, Professor Adams pointed the way for later critics such as Casalduero,[12] Pujals,[13] Marrast[14] and Antón Andrés,[15] suggesting where the real worth of the novel lay. Sancho Saldaña, far from being a Scottian optimist confident of his own strength, is closer to the disillusioned Byronian figure that was Larra.[16] We come to learn then from these other critics how Espronceda, already at this early stage in his career and in the rigid format which the historical novel genre presupposes, infused so much of himself and his romantic credo in these characters and their aspirations. Sancho Saldaña struggles unsuccessfully through life, bringing misery and death upon the woman he loves, Leonor, and those who love him, Elvira, his sister, and Zoraida the passionately jealous lover.

The most interesting part of *Sancho Saldaña* lies in the development of the melancholy character of its protagonist and his hopeless career, the growing disenchantment with life and his disdainful withdrawal from society.[17] Equally admirable are the vivid descriptions of landscapes, vignettes of local color and the portraits of life in feudal times, such as castles, country fairs, jousts, etc.

The plot, though replete with sub-plot upon sub-plot, mainly follows the love story between two members of rich and powerful families, Sancho Saldaña and Leonor de Iscar. The two clans part ways when the Saldañas become supporters of the King Sancho IV and the Iscars backers of the La Cerda brothers who are pretenders to the throne. Momentarily smitten by the beautiful Jewess Zoraida, Saldaña later regains his senses but when he comes to ask for Leonar's hand, her father Don Jaime de Iscar refuses to give consent for the marriage and the emnity between the families takes a turn for the worse. Upon the death of Don Jaime, Saldaña engages the services of «El Velludo» and his band of outlaws to kidnap Leonor, a charge they carry out with success. As a result Hernando de Iscar, her brother, challenges Saldaña to a duel to the death. Leonor, an innocent victim of Hernando's unbendable code of honor, is torn between saving her brother's life and marrying Saldaña. In the end she herself dies resignedly, as does Zoraida, consumed by jealousy and vengeance, and Elvira, Sancho's own sister, tormented by her brother's crimes.

The plot is conventional in that none of the dozens of incidents can be said to cause surprise. At the same time, while it does not precisely resemble any other specific historical novel, it is not very different from most. The *de rigeur* secret passages, concealed doors, torture chambers, treasons, assassinations, moonlight nights, storms, conspiracies, witchcraft and other inescapable ingredients are all here.[18] The characterization is for the most part weak with the already noted exception of Sancho Saldaña.

Neither the historical nor the fictional characters are animated by more than a few psychological strokes, though more often they are recognized by some phrase they are fond of uttering or other physical trait repeated throughout the entirety of the novel. The style is often ponderous in the narrative passages, flowery in the descriptive ones and stilted when it comes to the dialogued portions. The only relief here are the interpolated poems of which «A una dama burlada» and «La cautiva» later found their way into the volume of *Poesías* (1840). The themes of love (Saldaña's senseless passion for Leonor, Zoraida's impossible love for Saldaña, Usdróbal's desire for Leonor and Jimeno's lust for Zoraida), revenge (Abraham's for Judaism's oppressors, the Iscar's hate for the Saldaña's), honor (the novel's second letimotiv especially insofar as it affects Hernando de Iscar), freedom (Espronceda's lifelong preoccupation, reflected here primarily as a conflict between a king and a blood pretender to the throne), Nature alive (raging storms, lugubrious settings, mysterious occurrences) all give rise to innumerable episodes that needlessly complicate the main plot and make the reading tiresome.[19]

Lack of cohesion and interest is the most often voiced objection to *Sancho Saldaña*—Espronceda's alledged unpremeditated plan and hurried composition. Such carelessness has on occasion resulted in the charge that, more than a novel, the work is simply a succession of loosely tied episodes, slow-paced, populated by flat characters who are animated by «literary» emotions and written in a repetitive style. This would seem to be the most negative sort of criticism that could be levelled against *Sancho Saldaña*. But while the work may not contribute anything new to the historical novel—itself a genre suspect of belletristic worth—, *Sancho Saldaña* testifies to what a first-rate creative mind could do with such a stilted and lifeless genre. Cervantes' experience with a comparably museum-like genre, the pastoral novel, and his own contribution to it in the form of *La Galatea* would, I believe, serve as a parallel case. Neither author has suffered posthumously for having tried his hand at it. Espronceda's projection of himself in the rebel Byronian hero that is Saldaña, the disenchantment with life that dooms all of the protagonists, the apologue on behalf of the populace who struggle against an inert and decadent aristocracy, an idearium of his own literary culture and the foreshadowing samples of what his lyric poetry was to become all add up to a substantial reason why, if not the general reader, at least the student of nineteenth century Spanish literature should find Espronceda's *Sancho Saldaña* profitable reading.

III. Essays and Brief Narratives

If in *Sancho Saldaña* and later in his poetry Espronceda managed to convey a great deal of personal sentiment, the genuinely felt *tedium vitae* resultant from the constant disillusionment that reality presents to every romantic when it falls short of his expectations, in the shorter narrative and essayistic works we find a straightforward and unabashed representation of his economic, social, governmental and literary ideas. It is in this lesser known dimension, his essayistic production, that Espronceda comes across as an informed, concerned and active individual in the real world of national politics. Unfortunately many have discounted the ideals and the programs he advocated, thinking him an irresponsible, irrepresible rebel out of touch with workaday solutions to the crises and problems facing Spain in the years he lived. A closer look, however, at his newspaper and magazine articles or at the congressional record of the *Cortes* (Spanish Parliament) where he gave five speeches (March-May 1842) throws a very different kind of light on this young, articulate and dedicated citizen. The seriousness and the committment evinced throughout, though devoid of the mordant sarcasm, often call to mind the writings of his friend Mariano José de Larra. Larra may be the most representative socio-political romantic thinker of the times; certainly, he was the most influential of his day. Espronceda, equally well-known, did not lag far behind in effectiveness and sincerity.

The twenty-some short pieces left behind by Espronceda[20] fit five categories according to theme or subject matter. A) Political essays and speeches: «Influencia del gobierno sobre la poesía,» *El Siglo* (28 February 1834); «Libertad. Igualdad. Fraternidad.,» *El Español* (15 January 1836); «El gobierno y la bolsa,» *El Español* (7 March 1836); *El ministerio Mendizábal,* Imp. de Repullés (April 1836); «Política general,» *El Pensamiento* (19 May 1841); «Política general,» *El Pensamiento* (July 1841); and five speeches delivered in the Spanish Parliament touching on the issues of taxes, import quotas, laws governing the press and the church, military preparedness, and the draft. B) Literary topics: four theatre reviews, «Crónica de teatros,» n.d.; «Teatros,» *El Artista* (no. 17, 1835); «*Teatros. Alfredo*. Drama original en cinco actos por don Joaquín Pacheco.» n.d.; «Seducción y venganza o *El marido inglés,*» *El Artista* (no. 22, 1835); the comparative study «Estudio crítico de *La Jerusalén,* del Tasso y *La Henriada,* de Voltaire,» published for the first time by Philip H. Churchman in the *Revue Hispanique*, volume 17, 1907; «Poesía,» *El Siglo* (24 January 1834); and «El pastor Clasiquino,» *El Artista* (24 May 1935). C) Autobiographical accounts: «Un recuerdo,» *El Pensamiento* (June 1841);

«De Gibraltar a Lisboa. Viaje Histórico,» *El Pensamiento* (August 31, 1841). D) A short story: «La pata de palo,» *El Artista* (22 march 1835). E) An article of customs and manners: «Costumbres,» *El Artista* (no. 26, 1835).[21]

IV. Short Fiction and Autobiographical Accounts

Curiously enough, even though strictly speaking Espronceda wrote the one short story, «La pata de palo,» to date just one lone critical study has been dedicated to it[22] since its date of publication in 1835.[23] With hyperbole and good humor Espronceda begins his tale establishing a jocose tone where linguistic and situational irony take place side by side (e.g., «escarmentar en *pierna* ajena» instead of *cabeza* or «mis piernas están a su disposición»). The story, which takes place in London, tells of a very rich businessman who had the misfortune of breaking a leg so «perfectly» that surgeons could not mend it and had been forced to amputate it. Undaunted and almost eagerly the cripple called to his home a famous manufacturer of wooden legs, a Mr. Wood (irony, once again, that went unappreciated by most Spaniards, one supposes), and entrusted him with coming up with the best wooden leg he had ever produced; it should be even better than the real one, capable of carrying the whole body, of walking by itself. Two days later, on a beautiful May morning, the prosthesis is delivered to the expectant recipient by a clerk of Mr. Wood's who claims that his master has really outdone himself, having turned out the most perfect example of a wooden leg. As if to prove the young man's words correct, the merchant has hardly fitted his new member, when the leg of its own accord and under its own vigorous and unstoppable power carries the helpless, forty-year-old overweight cripple around the house totally beyond his control. Scantily dressed, the poor man soon finds himself out of his house, then out of his neighborhood, London, England, and, as the years pass and his ailing body struggles to keep up with the rebellious wooden leg, he is thought to have been seen criss-crossing the Candian woods and more recently, as a dismembering skeleton still impelled by the most perfect example of Mr. Wood's craft, climbing the Pyrenees mountain range.

The last words of the story, underlined by Espronceda himself, «*movimiento perpetuo*,» with which he characterizes the machine-like prosthesis perhaps serve to uncover what Espronceda was ridiculing. The idle dreams of scientists hoping to find such a machine awakened in the writer a humorous notion that he converted into a fanciful tale to the discomfiture of some.

Unfortunately, as Professor Vasari has discovered,[24] the story is not an original one of Espronceda's. Under the title «Mynheer von Wodenblock, A Marvellous History,» there appeared in the journal *The Polar Star* in 1830—five years before «La pata de palo»—the same tale in English.[25] Only a few changes were made by Espronceda. Rotterdam becomes London, the protagonist's name is different and the circumstances under which the wealthy businessman broke his leg differ a little. A second version, this one in French, was published in the *Revue de Paris* in the same year. And finally in 1832 a third version appeared in the *Revue étrangère* (Saint-Pétersbourg) also in French. Espronceda, who had spent almost the totality of his years of exile (1827-1833) in England and France, had ample opportunity to read one if not more of these tales before he translated it into his own Spanish version. The process is surely reminiscent of the one earlier uncovered by Vicente Lloréns[26] relating to Espronceda's poem «Despedida del patriota griego de la hija del apóstata» and the English original «The Patriot and the Apostate's Daughter, or the Greek Lover's Farewell,» discussed previously in Chapter Three.[27]

The only two autobiographical pieces known, each averaging somewhat less than six pages, concern his period of exile. «Un recuerdo» recalls the nostalgia felt when as a refugee, Espronceda contemplated his misfortune on a warm August evening on the outskirts of London. Walking about the country estate of his father's friend, Lord Ruthwen, the young and melancholy emigrè dwells on everything dear but forbidden to him because of being distanced from his country due to irreconcilable political ideals. The second narrative, «De Gibraltar a Lisboa. Viaje histórico,» looks further back into the past when as a seventeen-year-old Espronceda left his home and his country to see the world and escape the suffocating political climate which predominated under Fernando VII. «De Gibraltar a Lisboa,» generally considered to be the best among Espronceda's short prose writings, like «Un recuerdo,» was written many years after the occurrence of these events. This is noticeable not only in the natural fluidity and liveliness of the style but also in those instances where a comparison between the «then» and the «now» comes through as in the sentence, «Yo, que tenía entonces muchas más ilusiones por las mujeres que tengo ahora...».

There is humor in the recounting of his boat trip from the English port of Gibraltar to Lisbon but, unlike the near hysterical tone purposely used for satirical effect in «La pata de palo,» Espronceda here employs an almost benevolent and endearing humor sympathetic to the travails of an inexperienced and perhaps slightly foolish young man beginning his adventure in life without fully realizing it. «De Gibraltar a Lisboa» looks back fondly and with some pride to an earlier age when the poet broke away unhesitatingly from the comfort and the security afforded him by his family's position, trading it for the uncertainties of a life whose only assured benefit would be freedom. This was a choice that Espronceda continued to make the rest of his life. He sacrificed everything to freedom for as long as it was needed.

The narration of the four- or five-day crossing, taking place in mid-August of 1827, is filled with colorful details, vivid descriptions and a retrospective good humor. Twenty-nine passengers and a crew of four, crowded into a small fishing sloop, endure a perilous storm on the third day of the journey, which includes a woman's death, unsavory food in the form of salted cod with rice seasoned with garlic and hot peppers, the sickening drink of gin and tepid water, and fights brought about by the lack of space and the dastardly conditions. The final sentence, «...nos pidieron no sé que dinero. Y saqué un duro, único que tenía, y me devolvieron dos pesetas, que arrojé al río Tajo, porque no quería entrar en tan gran capital con tan poco dinero.», tells of the grand gesture of a destitute, bearded young rebel at which, as an older narrator, Espronceda must have been proud and pleased.

V. Political Pamphlets

Not unexpectedly the largest number of essays written by Espronceda are those dealing with political questions, closely followed by articles on literary topics. As should be obvious by now, politics and literature were his life's coordinates, so when the titles surface in which both disciplines appear (*e.g.*, «Influencia del gobierno sobre la poesía»), the reader can not be too surprised. In cases similar to the example just cited, Espronceda's allegiance remains undisputably on the side of literature, feeling that «la independencia es mejor musa que la protección.»

«Libertad. Igualdad, Fraternidad.» inaugurates a collection of serious political and social essays advocating reforms that governments in general, and particularly the Spanish government, can and should undertake for the benefit of the nation and its citizens. Building on the principles of the French sociologist Claude Henri de Saint-Simon and the Englishman Robert Owen, Espronceda expounds on the idea that man's freedom should be limited solely by his abilities.[28] On an idealistic but viable tack

Espronceda proposes that those privileges accorded to an individual by birth (*i.e.,* social status, economic wealth, etc.) be discounted in the role he is to play in society or the station he hopes to attain in life. The possibility must be open to every man to achieve his highest goal so long as talent and intellectual worth are the only criteria required. The three ideals named in the title compose an interlocking system through which one underpins and serves, in turn, to secure the others. The danger, once more, as the poem «Canción del pirata» (see Chapter Four) illustrated earlier, results when these ideals are carried to their logical conclusion. For, if an individual's liberty is so total, it can not but infringe on the rights of another and consequently on the rights—i.e., laws—of society as a whole.

The most celebrated of Espronceda's strictly political papers were written about, and mostly against, the Prime Minister Juan Alvarez de Mendizábal who governed Spain in the eight months between September 14, 1835 and May 15, 1836. Mendizábal came to power as a liberal politician bent on dispelling the dictatorial atmosphere that the governments of Fernando VII and the Count of Toreno had brought about in the country. Espronceda, like many other liberals, enthusiastically endorsed and initially worked on behalf of Mendizábal's candidacy, so that when the new Prime Minister took office, the poet became an official political appointee undertaking a delicate mission in the region of Andalucía to the south. Once in power, however, Mendizábal found how difficult it was to put into effect many of the reforms for which he had campaigned and that he, as well as his supporters, had expected to become reality. As a consequence, support for his government began to wane and the discontent with its policies grew steadily louder.

Espronceda's opening shot in the anti-Mendizábal campaign took the form of the article «El gobierno y la bolsa.» This salvo accused the government of equating the welfare of the nation with a high stock market index and of endeavoring to perpetrate this false standard as an incontrovertible truth for all Spaniards. So single-minded is this pursuit, Espronceda contends, that it would not be far-fetched to see the government in terms of a corporation, so that, instead of a prime minister, Mendizábal (who is never mentioned by name) would truly function as the chairman of the board. Espronceda criticizes the methods through which the government means to achieve national prosperity and enduring political union. The stock market should neither be the way to achieve this goal, nor the index by which to gauge its success.

The most instrumental weapon in helping to bring about the downfall of the Mendizábal government, however, had to be Espronceda's twenty-four page pamphlet (Madrid: Delgado, Abril 1836) titled *El ministerio*

Mendizábal. Quite apparently Espronceda's disenchantment had reached the point where anonymity of the accused was no longer a consideration. Headed by a quote taken from Larra's essay «Dios nos asista,» also an indictment of the same government, where Figaro says: «Aquí llaman esto un *Gobierno* representativo, ..., confieso que yo llamo esto un *hombre representativo,*»²⁹ the pamphlet was widely circulated and applauded even though the censors toned down and expurgated several of the most damaging passages. Many newspapers and magazines carried excerpts from *El ministerio Mendizábal,* indicating how popular it became.

The main thrust of this long essay is directed once more at Mendizábal's unsound and—to Espronceda's mind—almost unprincipled fiscal policies, though, to be sure, the government was also chastized for the loss of faith and confidence in which it had incurred as a result of inaction and lack of sufficient change. On February 16 and 19, and March 8 of 1836, the Mendizábal government had issued a decree which thereafter became known as «*desamortización.*» Through this proclamation, all of the Church properties were expropriated by the government which, in turn, became obligated to pay a salary to the clergy and other religious factions since their communities—including the Jesuits'—were declared dissolved.

Neither Espronceda nor most of his liberal friends appear particularly opposed to this policy of «*desamortización*»; what troubled them was the government's follow-through plan. The vast Church landholdings were put up for sale at very low prices but the government provisos which dictated these sales favored their purchase mainly by government bond holders and speculators. The small farmers who most needed the additional agricultural fields derived minimal benefit from the «*desamortización,*» while the wealthy farmers, owners of huge *latifundios* or large estates became even more wealthy at the expense of the Church and of the small farmers for whom it should have been intended. Espronceda wanted «*desamortización*» to be part of a comprehensive agrarian reform package, a more equitable, farsighted and durable plan in which those who worked the land—and not just held it as real estate—were to realize the benefits of low prices, tax credits, price supports, etc. As it turned out, the extant inequality between the haves and the have-nots grew to a greater disparity. Economic inequality breeds social inequality and in turn, political inequality which ultimately affects freedom at every level—an unforgettable, indeed a sacred principle for Espronceda who wrote about it and fought for it all of his life.

The efficacy and power of the press was amply demonstrated for the first time in Spain, when one month after the publication of Larra's and

Espronceda's articles, Juan Alvarez Mendizábal was forced to step down as Prime Minister.

VI. Literary Writings

Although Espronceda remained an active participant in the world of letters until the very end, he does not show an overly keen interest in the academic or critical study of literature. The number of essays treating literary subjects he produced is less than half of those dedicated to items of a political, social or economic nature. Espronceda's lack of enthusiasm for poetics can be gauged by his attitude towards his appointment to a lectureship in modern comparative literature by the Liceo Artístico y Literario. The nomination in March, 1839, coming from the Madrid cultural society resulted in one only lecture, remembered as rambling and unstructured by his friend Enrique Gil y Carrasco.[30] Espronceda did, of course, write the obligatory theater reviews. Some, for example, «Seducción y venganza o *El marido inglés*» went no further than half a dozen lines, and most were dashed off without regard for any but initial momentary reactions to a dramatic performance.

In what is probably one of Espronceda's first published essays on the theme of literature, «Poesía,» he upholds the romantic school as a new wave in literature whose time has come. It is a comparison-contrast between Classicism and Romanticism where literary canons, such as the drama's three unities, are held in ridicule as impediments for writing in a modern fashion. Significantly enough, neither politics nor the theme of freedom remains absent from this two-page essay. The penultimate sentence in «Poesía,» «En política como en poesía, la perfección está en conciliar el mayor grado de libertad con el mayor grado de orden posible,» demonstrates well that Espronceda did not believe in a «pure» literary essay. He espoused a credo of literary activism where none of the four genres should exist in a rarified atmosphere as mere bellestristic curiosities. Whether writing as a creator of fiction and poetry or as an author of critical writings, Espronceda rarely failed to make life part of his art.

The essay «Estudio crítico de la *Jerusalén,* del Tasso y *La Henriada,* de Voltaire» is as close as Espronceda came to a literary essay devoid of ancillary or extrinsic preoccupations. This three page commentary written around 1828-30,[31] unpublished in the author's lifetime,[32] is written in an epistolary fashion and does not carry a title other than the generic one cited and assigned to it by the critics through the years. The article reflects the lessons learned by Espronceda from his master Alberto Lista, though his own preferences as a budding romantic poet show through clearly. In his critical study Espronceda praises the Italian Torcuato Tasso as the greatest modern poet, save perhaps for Ludovico Ariosto whose *Orlando Furioso* he knew well,[33] while chastizing Voltaire for having criticized so harshly the former's masterpiece *Gerusalemme Liberata*. He prefers the vigor and harmony of Tasso's verse to the rational coldness of Voltaire's measured prose. Declaring with obvious hyperbole to have read «one thousand times» slowly and admiringly Tasso's Renaissance epic, Espronceda damns Voltaire by claiming that the reading of *La Henriade* was laborious and boring to the point of nearly making him fall asleep.

Espronceda's most famous literary article is the satire «El pastor Clasiquino,» a one page attack against the neoclassic school of lyric poetry. «Clasiquino» is a derivation of the pejorative word «clasiquista» coined by Eugenio Ochoa,[34] co-founder of the journal *El Artista* where Espronceda published his piece, to designate the stereotyped and traditional classicist advocate, resistant to all innovation in the arts and in literature. The success of this little essay rests on Espronceda's masterful parody of all of the better-known literary recourses used by the neoclassic authors in their writings, primarily in their poetry: the peaceful bucolic setting, the shepherd lamenting his beloved's disdain, the babbling brook where the flock drinks crystalline water, the metaphors («pregnant machine» meaning canon, «sonorous tube» meaning trumpet) are ridiculed along with the figure of a neoclassic poet who, while adjusting his spectacles muses about eclogues and onomatopoeias, and who seeks to follow Aristotle's teachings upon improving on reality so as to make Nature as she should be and not as she actually is. The poetry of his near contemporary Juan Meléndez Valdés (1754-1817) who wrote in an imitative style of Garcilaso de la Vega's (1501-1536) Renaissance pastoral lyrics is held to ridicule as the paradigm of what Espronceda considers risible when three of his verses are quoted, plus one of his model's, and woven into the satirical narrative. In the final sentence, by means of a play on words («*borrego*» sheep, but also meaning «simpleton» in slang), Clasiquino, the likely civil servant who would be a poet, returns to his fold determined to remain a sheep as long as he lives. Espronceda in «El pastor Clasiquino» is never better in the use of humor, parody and learned negative criticism of the adversaries of Romanticism, the die-hard practitioners of the neoclassical mode at an age when their time was clearly past.

NOTES

1. E. Allison Peers, «Studies in the Influence of Sir Walter Scott in Spain,» *Revue Hispanique*, 68 (October 1926), 57.

2. Robert Marrast, *José de Espronceda: El Estudiante de Salamanca. El Diablo Mundo* (Madrid: Castalia, 1978), p. 354.

3. E. Allison Peers, *Historia del movimiento romántico español*, Vol. I (Madrid: Gredos, 1954), pp. 239-240 erroneously lists only three novels, forgetting López Soler's work.

4. Ricardo Navas-Ruiz, *El Romanticismo Español* (Salamanca: Anaya, 1970), p. 169.

5. See Allison Peers' essay cited above, footnote 1, and Nicholson B. Adams, «Notes on Espronceda's *Sancho Saldaña*,» *Hispanic Review*, 5 (October 1937), 304-308.

6. Philip H. Churchman and E. Allison Peers, «A Survey of the Influence of Sir Walter Scott in Spain,» *Revue Hispanique*, 65 (1922), 268-310. E. Allison Peers, see above footnote no. 1.

7. E. Allison Peers, article cited above in footnote no. 1, pp. 41-42.

8. M.B. Travis «The Influence of Walter Scott on Espronceda's *Sancho Saldaña*.» M.A. thesis cited by Allison Peers, *op.cit.*, p. 41 ff.

9. Allison Peers, *op. cit.*, p. 69.

10. N.B. Adams, *op. cit.*, (see above footnote 5), p. 305.

11. Adams, *ibid.*, p. 306.

12. Joaquín Casalduero, *Espronceda* (Madrid, 1967), pp. 249-59.

13. Esteban Pujals, *Espronceda y Lord Byron* (Madrid, 1972), pp. 144-48.

14. Marrast, *op. cit.*, pp. 353-383.

15. Angel Antón Andrés in the «Prólogo» to his edition of José de Espronceda, *Sancho Saldaña o El Castellano de Cuéllar*, 2 vols. (Barcelona: Barral Editores, 1974), pp. 7-42.

16. Adams, *op. cit.*, pp. 305, 307.

17. Antón Andrés, *op. cit.*, p. 29.

18. For a much longer and more complete catalog of romantic accessories see Casalduero, *op. cit.*, p. 253.

19. Marrast, *op. cit.*, p. 356 and especially Antón Andrés upon whose introduction I base my paragraph (*op. cit.*, pp. 36-38) will provide the reader with a more extensive treatment of the subject.

20. R. Marrast., *Espronceda, articles et discours oubliés. La bibliothèque d'Espronceda (d'apres un document inédit)*. Paris: Presses Uni. de France, 1966. This thin booklet contains a wealth of information regarding the lesser known pieces of Espronceda.

21. Of all of the titles given here, sixteen are reproduced in complete form in Jorge Campos' edition *Obras completas de D. José de Espronceda,* Biblioteca de Autores Españoles, vol. 72 (Madrid: Atlas, 1954), pp. 573-608. See Marrast, footnote above, for nine additional reprintings.

22. Stephen Vasari, «'La pata de palo.' Fuente y sentido de un cuento de Espronceda.» *Papeles de Son Armadans,* 65 (1972), 49-56.

23. Espronceda published it a second time in the magazine *No me olvides,* 23 (8 October 1837), pp. 1-3.

24. Vasari, *op. cit.,* pp. 51-53.

25. Vasari, *ibid.,* p. 51, also notes that this story in its English version, according to a note in *The Polar Star*, had appeared previously in 1926 and «had been copied in many newspapers, even in Calcutta.»

26. V. Lloréns, «El original inglés de una poesía de Espronceda,» *Nueva Revista de Filología Hispánica* 5 (1951),418-22.

27. I fail to see an implied moral or message other than the suggested one of laughing at the notion of a perpetual motion machine. And, while I recognize the worth of Mr. Vasari's essay, I do not share his hypothesis that the story may be a veiled critique of political or financial manipulations of the times.

28. David J. Billick, «Espronceda, ensayista,» *Abside,* 42 (1978), p. 346. R. Marrast, *op. cit.,* 519, 520, 528, 529.

29. Mariano José Larra (Fígaro), «Dios nos asista,» *BAE,* Vol., 128 (Madrid, 1960), p. 196.

30. Cited in José de Espronceda, *Poesías líricas y fragmentos épicos,* Robert Marrast, ed. (Madrid, 1970), p. 20.

31. Marrast, *op. cit.,* p. 193.

32. First published by Enrique Rodríguez Solís, *Espronceda. Su tiempo, su vida y sus obras* (Madrid, 1883), pp. 88-90. A second, more faithful transcription from the Biblioteca Nacional (Madrid) manuscript (Number 18633[29]) was done by Philip H. Churchman, «Espronceda. More Inedita,» *Revue Hispanique,* 17 (1907), 707-10.

33. See Churchman *op. cit.,* p. 708.

34. Eugenio Ochoa, «Un romántico,» *El Artista* (18 January 1835), p. 36.

CHAPTER NINE

Summation

José de Espronceda was an extraordinary man who lived in Spain in the worst of times. Born on the eve of the Napoleonic invasion and the War of Independence, he endured the despotic rule of Fernando VII and died as the Carlist conflict simmered in Navarra and the Basque provinces. Nevertheless, Espronceda achieved marked success in the parallel walks of life he chose for himself—literature and politics.

His first poem, now lost, «Al 7 de julio,» was written at the age of fifteen; his first novel, *Sancho Saldaña,* at twenty-five and his most celebrated verses compositions, the «Canciones», were well known by the time Espronceda reached his twenty-seventh year. Though brief by any standard, Espronceda's existence was full, fruitful and influential beyond his premature death at the age of thirty-four. His legacy to the realm of Spanish letters is primarily contained in a slim collection of poems, *Poesías* (1840) and in the two longer verse works *El Estudiante de Salamanca* (1840) and *El Diablo Mundo* (1840-42). And though the significance attached to these poetic writings might seem disproportionate, Espronceda cultivated all four literary genres in additional works. The plays *Ni el tío ni el sobrino* (1834), *Amor venga sus agravios* (1838) and *Blanca de Borbón* (1870), the novel *Sancho Saldaña* (1834) and the various political, literary, narrative and autobiographical essays produced throughout his mature years attest to Espronceda's genuine dedication to the romantic aesthetic. But neither as dramatist, novelist, nor essayist did Espronceda excel to the extent that he succeeded as a poet. In this genre he stands alone as the finest among Spanish Romantics.

Educated under the stern neoclassical tutorship of Alberto Lista, Espronceda acquired early the prerequisites of a true poet by learning from the verses of the Greek and the Latin poets. Equally part of his apprenticeship were the classic Spanish poets such as Herrera, Garcilaso, Jorge

Manrique, and the neoclassics Quintana and Meléndez Valdés. On his own, Espronceda learned English and French and from these two cultures he drew on the writings of those authors who best exemplified his own spiritual bent, Ossian, Lord Byron, Walter Scott, Ronsard and Béranger. Espronceda's formative period concluded with the assimilation of all of these disparate sources around 1833, the year he returned to Spain from self-exile in France and England. Now ideologically secure as well as technically experienced Espronceda produced in the space of five years (1835-1840) all of the poems upon which his stature as the foremost romantic poet rests. These are only a handful, at most half a dozen relatively short compositions: «Canción del pirata,» «El mendigo,» «El verdugo,» and «El reo de muerte» all dating from 1835, «A Jarifa en una orgía» (1837), and the «Canto a Teresa» (1839-40). The longer *El Estudiante de Salamanca* (1840), though written in verse form is truly a dramatic poem, more theatrical than lyrical, whose influence has been primarily theatrical as Zorrilla's *Don Juan Tenorio* evinces in the opening scenes of Act I and in the character of the protagonist.

Espronceda could be all things as a writer so wide were his interests, so ample his talents and so complete the mastery of his craft. In *El Diablo Mundo* he demonstrated a supreme poetic arrogance in touching a theme as grand as one could imagine (the history of mankind) and by producing it in installments that bore out his heuristic gifts. In the «Canción del pirata» and the remaining «Canciones» Espronceda inaugurated a new poetic lexicon and a form/content schemata that revolutionized the way poetry was to be written thereafter in the Spanish language—neither Bécquer nor the Generation of 1898 nor even the poetry of the following Generation of 1927 is conceivable without Espronceda's «Canciones» cycle. In *El Estudiante de Salamanca* Espronceda appropriated one of the most deeply rooted Spanish literary figures, that of Don Juan, and, while retaining its most characteristic and recognizable traits, managed to instill in it the satanic proportions of a titan. In *Sancho Saldaña* he simply reached into the Christian medieval world of Spanish history and Walter Scott's legendary and adventuresome rendition of the epoch and composed his own historical and romantic potboiler. In the theater his best effort, *Blanca de Borbón*, once again shows an eclecticism which combines classical adherence to the three unities, grandeur of the characters, formal versification, and a contrapuntal innovativeness reflected in the subservience of reason to passion, the cherished ideal of liberty and the tone and movement of each scene. And yet in every one of the cited instances, meant not only to illustrate but to symbolize the whole of his production, Espronceda managed to imprint his unmistakable seal of an individual profoundly convinced that illusions and

ideals, though indispensable to every man, must bow in the face of com-
monplace reality.

The ideals implicit in his verse and fictional works were espoused
fervently and openly by Espronceda at all times as a citizen. His role in the
social and political spheres, though commonly disregarded if only because
of his literary stardom, was that of an activist who, by any means at his
disposal, pursued an unwavering dedication on behalf of individual liberty.
Beginning as a fifteen-year-old youngster, upon witnessing the public execution of the liberal General Riego in 1823, Espronceda's other
career—his political one—was initiated with the founding of the secret
society of «Los Numantinos» whose avowed purpose—signed in
blood—was the overthrow of the absolutist Fernando VII. A dissolution of
the conspirators' club and a five-year sentence handed down to its co-
founder put an end to this first show of resistance to tyranny. Unable to
bear the heavy hand of Fernando VII's police rule and desirous to seek
adventure in more propitious climates, Espronceda embarked at Gibraltar
on a journey of self-exile that would take him to Portugal, Great Britain,
France, Belgium and other parts of Europe where he forged his ideals of
liberty and equality. At times he fought for others, as was the case in
famous July weeks of 1830 Paris barricades, and at other times he sought
to sabotage the rule of Fernando VII, as when he joined Colonel Joaquín
de Pablo «Chapalangarra» and his handful of rebels in Navarra in an incursion across the Pyrenees where de Pablo was shot to death and the rest
of his followers barely escaped with their lives. Only when amnesty was
declared by the Spanish Regent María Cristina for all political exiles, five
years after he had left his country, did Espronceda consider returning to
Spain. By the time he found himself back in Madrid, in March of 1833, his
father had died, Fernando VII no longer ran the country and the influx of
liberals and Romantics was changing the life of the capital. A careless
reading in public of some derrogatory verses referring to the ailing King
ended Espronceda's career as a member of the Corps of Royal Guards and
resulted in his banishment from Madrid. There were other times when anti-
government zealousness or too-spirited a defense of political or social
ideals resulted in nights spent in jail, but following Fernando's death in
September of 1833 Espronceda's political fortunes became less turbulent
and quite likely more rewarding. Only once again in the summer of 1834
was he sent away from the Spanish capital, this time to Badajoz by the
Martínez de la Rosa government.

Espronceda's literary standing went hand-in-hand with his reformed
political attitudes. In June of 1836 he became a candidate for the Spanish
Parliament from the province of Almería. Unsuccessful, he tried again the

following year from Granada. Earlier he had undertaken a delicate political mission as an official envoy of the Mendizábal government, a government he did so much to help gain power and one he managed to see driven from power by dint of his most celebrated political essay *El ministerio Mendizábal*. A third time Espronceda sought and failed to achieve election to Parliament from the province of Badajoz in 1838. Undaunted, he continued to work on behalf of those political figures and programs that most clearly resembled his own. Espronceda, now operating within a more narrow and accepted political context, slowly became aware of the need to build a power base from which to operate and as a result began to tour cities and provinces in a campaign to meet with political bosses asking for their support and financial backing.

It was not until the abdication of the Regent María Cristina that Espronceda finally realized his ambition to occupy a place inside the government. When the liberal General Baldomero Espartero came to power in May of 1841, Espronceda was appointed secretary to the Spanish embassy in the Low Countries, a nomination likely made as payment for Espronceda's written and active support for the next Regent. The poet had scarcely time to settle in his newly appointed post (a few days), when he received word that he had at last been elected to Parliament as Representative from the province of Almería. Returning promptly from the Hague, on March 1, 1842, he took his seat for the first time in the Spanish *Cortes*. Though, understandably, the press reported a tentativeness in his initial behavior, Espronceda soon became an active participant in the chamber's deliberations. Aside from the casual, extemporaneous daily remarks, in the three months (March through May 1842) he served in the *Cortes* he left behind five parliamentary speeches which reflect a range of interests that encompass everything from import quotas to the military draft.

Both his political and his literary careers were cut short by an untimely death when, as a congressman and as the author of *El Diablo Mundo*, Espronceda had prospects of unlimited success before him in his two chosen paths of life—literature and politics.

SELECTED BIBLIOGRAPHY

PRIMARY SOURCES

Listed below are the principal editions of Espronceda's major works. I have omitted unauthorized, limited and special issue editions of which there were many in the last quarter of the nineteenth century and in the first part of the 1900s. The first comprehensive Espronceda bibliography was Philip H. Churchman's «An Espronceda Bibliography,» *Revue Hispanique*, 17 (1907), 741-73. More up to date is David J. Billick's *José de Espronceda: An Annotated Bibliography, 1834-1980* (New York: Garland Publishing, Inc. 1981).

Sancho Saldaña, o El Castellano de Cuéllar. Novela histórica del Siglo XIII. 6 vol. Madrid: Imprenta de Repullés, 1834.
Ni el tío ni el sobrino. Madrid: Imprenta de Repullés, 1834. Espronceda's second play written in collaboration with Antonio Ros de Olano.
Amor venga sus agravios. Madrid: Imprenta de D. José María de Repullés, 1838. Espronceda's third play written in collaboration with Eugenio Moreno López.
Poesías de D. José de Espronceda. Madrid: Imprenta de Yenes, 1840. The first collection of Espronceda's poetry. Does not include «Al Dos de Mayo» or *El Diablo Mundo*. Contains a prologue by José García de Villalta. Second edition in 1846; new printings in 1857 and 1874.
El Diablo Mundo, Poema de D. José de Espronceda. Madrid: Imp. de Boix, 1840-41. A serialized edition in two volumes and six cantos with a prologue by Antonio Ros de Olano. New printings in 1848 and 1849.
Obras poéticas de Don José de Espronceda, ed. Juan Eugenio de Hartzenbusch. Paris: Baudry («Colección de los Mejores Autores Españoles,» Vol. XLVI), 1848. Includes all of Espronceda's poems.

Reprintings in 1851, 1856, 1858, 1862, 1865, 1867, 1870 and 1879.

El Diablo Mundo. Poema de D. José de Espronceda. Madrid: Impr. de Gaspar y Roig, 1852. Contains an anonymous preface and several drawings of Bravo. Reprintings in 1861, 1865, 1869, 1872, 1875, 1880 and 1882.

Obras poéticas de Don José de Espronceda. Paris: Garnier, 1869. Reprintings in 1871, 1873, 1876, 1882, 1885, 1889, 1900, 1920 and 1923.

Sancho Saldaña o El Castellano de Cuéllar. Novela histórica original del siglo XIII. Segunda parte *de [*note that it does not say *por]* la de Don José de Espronceda. Tomo II. Madrid: J. Castro y Compañía, Editores, 1869. Inexplicably the first part seems to have been published secondly, and yet in the edition I consulted both parts appear, in the correct (if anachronistic) chronological order, bound into one single volume (!). This second volume is an apocryphal work, definitely not written by Espronceda. See *Sancho Saldaña* entry for 1974.

Sancho Saldaña. Tomo I. Madrid: J. Castro y Compañía, Editores, 1870. Philip H. Churchman, in his «An Espronceda Bibliography,» *Revue Hispanique*, 17 (1907), pp. 743-44, lists this entry and the above one as having been both published in 1869.

Páginas olvidadas de D. José de Espronceda. Madrid: Medina y Navarro, 1873. Contains prose and verse fragments unpublished until now; a prologue by Gumersindo Laverde. Reprintings in 1875 and 1882.

El Diablo Mundo, Poema de don José de Espronceda. Madrid: Perlado, Páez y Cía. («Colección de los Mejores Autores Antiguos y Modernos Nacionales y Extranjeros,» Tomo XIX), 1875. Reprintings in 1882, 1899, 1903, 1908, 1919 by the same publisher, and in 1924, 1932 and 1935 by Editorial Hernando.

El Estudiante de Salamanca, por D. José Espronceda. Madrid: Imprenta y Librería Roig, 1876. Illustrated and with an an anonymous prologue. Reprintings in 1881 and 1888.

Obras poéticas y escritos en prosa, eds. Patricio de la Escosura and Blanca Espronceda de Escosura. Madrid: Eduardo Mengíbar, 1884.

«Espronceda's *Blanca de Borbón*,» ed. Philip H. Churchman, *Revue Hispanique*, 17 (1907), 549-777. This is the second edition of Espronceda's finest play, yet to be staged. Its first edition, an extremely limited one done by Espronceda's daughter Blanca and annotated by her brother-in-law and the poet's friend Patricio de la Escosura, was published in 1870.

El Estudiante de Salamanca and other Selections, ed. George T. Northrup. Boston: Ginn and Co., 1919. Contains the «Canto a Teresa» and other poems besides a critical annotated version of the dramatic poem.

El Estudiante de Salamanca, ed. Edgar Allison Peers. Cambridge: University Press (Cambridge Plain Texts), 1922. 2nd printing in 1957.

Obras poéticas, ed. José Cascales Muñoz. Madrid: Rivadeneyra, 1923. Includes a biography of the poet, all of his previously published verse, even those compositions of doubtful parentage, and the play *Blanca de Borbón*.

Obras poéticas, I. Poesías y El estudiante de Salamanca, ed. José Moreno Villa. Madrid: La lectura («Clásicos Castellanos,» vol. 47), 1923. New, but identical, editions by Espasa-Calpe in 1933, 1942 and 1952.

Espronceda, II. El Diablo Mundo, ed. José Moreno Villa. Madrid: La Lectura («Clásicos Castellanos,» Vol. 50), 1923. Reprints by Espasa—Calpe in 1938, 1955 and 1965.

El auténtico Espronceda pornográfico y el apócrifo en general, ed. José Cascales Muñoz. Toledo: Imp. de Huérfanos, 1932. This slim volume contains an equal amount of critical material and the type of poetry described in the title. The scatological poem «Dido y Eneas,» written by Espronceda and his friend Miguel de los Santos Alvarez, is given preeminence.

Obras poéticas completas, ed. Juan José Domenchina. Madrid: Aguilar, 1936. Reprintings in 1942, 1945, 1951, 1959. The prologue by this poet of the Generation of 1927 includes a biographical sketch, an evaluation of Espronceda's works and a sonnet dedicated to him.

Obras completas, introd. Jorge Campos. Madrid: Atlas (Biblioteca de Autores Españoles, Vol. LXXII), 1954. Very comprehensive life and works prologue. Basic bibliography.

El Estudiante de Salamanca, ed. Carlos Beceiro, Madrid: Aguilar, 1965.

El Estudiante de Salamanca, ed. Benito Varela Jácome. Salamanca: Anaya («Textos Españoles,» Vol. 71), 1966. 2nd revised expanded ed. (Madrid: Ediciones Cátedra *[*«Letras Hispánicas»*]*), 1974.

El Diablo Mundo. El Estudiante de Salamanca. Poesías, ed. Jaime Gil de Biedma. Madrid: Alianza Editorial, 1966.

Poesías completas, ed. Juan Alcina Franch. Barcelona: Bruguera («Libro Clásico,» Vol. 47), 1968. Undistinguished introduction.

Poésies lyriques et fragments épiques, ed. Robert Marrast. Paris: Ed. Hispano-Americanas, 1969. First critical and chronological edition of Espronceda's poems and the «Pelayo.» Published in Spanish *Poesías líricas y fragmentos épicos*, ed. Robert Marrast. Madrid: Castalia («Clásicos Castalia,» Vol. 20), 1970. Excellent preliminary study.

El Estudiante de Salamanca, introd. Joaquín del Moral Ruiz. Madrid:
　　Libra, 1971.
Sancho Saldaña o El Castellano de Cuéllar, 2 vols., ed. Angel Antón An-
　　drés. Barcelona: Barral Editores, 1974. First critical edition of
　　Espronceda's only novel.
El Estudiante de Salamanca. *El Diablo Mundo*, ed. Robert Marrast. Ma-
　　drid: Castalia («Clásicos Castalia,» Vol. 81), 1978. The best and
　　most reliable edition of these two major works by Espronceda.

SECONDARY SOURCES

ADAMS, NICHOLSON B. «Notes on Espronceda's *Sancho Saldaña*.»
　　Hispanic Review, 5 (October 1937), 304-308. Further insights into Sir
　　Walter Scott's *Waverly* novels' influence on Espronceda's only ma-
　　jor fictional narrative.
BILLICK, DAVID J. «Espronceda ensayista.» *Abside,* 42 (1978), 337-51.
　　A much needed look at Espronceda's work as an essayist. The poet's
　　best-known nine essays and a passing reference to five speeches form
　　the basis for discussion in a socio-political context of Espronceda's
　　ideals.
　　_____. *José de Espronceda. An Annotated Bibliography, 1834-1980.*
　　New York: Garland Publishing, Inc. 1981.
BONILLA Y SAN MARTÍN, ADOLFO. «El pensamiento de
　　Espronceda.» *España Moderna,* 234 (June 1908), 69-101. An incisive
　　analysis of the poet's philosophical bent drawn from the doubts, the
　　angst and the pessimistic sentiments observed in some key poems.
　　Decidedly worthwhile.
CARNERO, GUILLERMO. *Espronceda.* Madrid: Ediciones Júcar, 1974.
　　This is a good popularizing volume that contains a lengthy introduc-
　　tion to the life and poetry of Espronceda. The second part of the
　　book is a well chosen selected anthology.
CASALDUERO, JOAQUÍN. *Espronceda.* Madrid: Editorial Gredos,
　　1961. A monograph in the life-and-works tradition. Subjective but
　　often insightful and perceptive. Lacks all critical apparatii.
　　_____. *Forma y visión de «El diablo mundo» de Espronceda.* Mad-
　　rid: Insula, 1951. An impressionistic, rambling and needlessly long,
　　running commentary of this verse work. Later (see above entry) con-
　　densed into a single chapter of the critic's *Espronceda.*
CASCALES MUÑOZ JOSÉ. *Don José de Espronceda: Su época, su vida*

y sus obras. Madrid: Biblioteca Hispania, 1914. One of the first and most useful of the life-times-and-works volumes on Espronceda. Contains valuable secondary sources and bibliographical items which can be put to good use.

CASTILLO, HOMERO. «Filosofía y arte de Espronceda.» *Hispania,* 34 (1951), 357-362. Short and perceptive appraisal of Espronceda's thought and its reflection in his poetry. More generalizing than Bonilla's and Landeira's on the same theme.

CASTRO, AMÉRICO. «Acerca de 'El diablo mundo' de Espronceda.» *Revista de Filología Española,* 7 (1920), 374-78. Brief treatment of Espronceda's longest verse work and its possible ascendancy in Voltaire's *L'Ingénu.* A suggestive and seminal note.

CHURCHMAN, PHILIP H. «An Espronceda Bibliography.» *Revue Hispanique,* 17 (1907), 741-73.

_____. «Byron and Espronceda.» *Revue Hispanique,* 29 (1909), 5-210. A thorough but subjective and, at times, biased examination of the shadow cast by Byron's poetry on Espronceda's verse. A good antidote is Esteban Pujals' (below) book on this same topic.

DREPS, JOSEPH A. «Was José de Espronceda an Innovator in Metrics?» *Philological Quarterly,* 18 (January 1939), 35-51. An affirmative reply, structured through analyses of individual verses, verse lines within strophes and strophes belonging to the same poem, is the conclusion drawn from this carefully reasoned essay.

FOSTER, DAVID WILLIAM. «A Note on Espronceda's Use of the *Romance* Meter in *El estudiante de Salamanca.*» *Romance Notes,* 7 (1965), 16-20. A brief but worthwhile look at Espronceda's use of this common meter and his chronological manipulation of the narrative sequence in the verse tale.

GARCÍA LORCA, FRANCISCO. «Espronceda y el paraíso.» *Romanic Review,* 43 (October 1952), 198-204. An excellent discussion of the philosophical needs of the poet and their ascertainable implications in his poetry.

HAFTER, MONROE Z. «'El diablo mundo' in the Light of Carlyle's 'Sartor Resartus'.» *Revista Hispánica Moderna,* 37 (1972-73), 46-55. Resemblances in the composition, structure and exposition of this unlikely pair shed light on the meaning of both works of satire and spiritual dissatisfaction.

HUTMAN, NORMA LOUISE. «Dos círculos en la niebla: 'El estudiante de Salamanca' y 'El diablo mundo'.» *Papeles de Son Armadans,* 59 (October 1970), 5-29. Well thought out analysis of these major works as examples of the essentially chaotic and fragmentary nature of the romantic concept of life and the universe.

ILIE, PAUL. «Espronceda and the Romantic Grotesque.» *Studies in Romanticism*, 11 (1972), 94-112. A thorough discussion of romantic grotesquerie and its presence in *El Diablo Mundo* and *El Estudiante de Salamanca*. A bibliographical gold-mine on the subject.

KING, EDMUND L. «What is Spanish Romanticism?» *Studies in Romanticism*, 2 (Autumn 1962), 1-11. A basic, well-organized historical and theoretical look at a key question in Spanish literature. Clear and useful.

LANDEIRA, RICARDO L. «La desilusión poética de Espronceda: Realidad y Poesía irreconciliables.» *Boletín de la Real Academia Española*, 55 (May-August 1975), 307-29. A reexamination of Espronceda's poetic credo through his political and sentimental lyrics that reveals the poet's inability to reconcile his aspirations with everyday reality and the resultant disillusionment and despair.

LLORÉNS CASTILLO, VICENTE. *Liberales y románticos. Una emigración española en Inglaterra (1823-1834)*, 2nd edition. Madrid: Editorial Castalia, 1968. An authoritative, well documented and reliable account of Spaniards in exile in England during the reign of Fernando VII. Interesting and very thorough.

_____. «El original inglés de una poesía de Espronceda.» *Nueva Revista de Filología Hispánica*, 5 (1951), 418-22. Documents the discovery of an anonymous English poem that Espronceda translated into his «La despedida del patriota griego de la hija del apóstata.» Reproduces the original 108-line poem «The Patriot and the Apostate's Daughter, or the Greek Lover's Farewell.»

MARRAST, ROBERT. *Espronceda. Articles et discours oubliés. La Bibliotèque d'Espronceda (d'après un document inédit)*. Paris: Presses Universitaires de France, 1966. A good source study for the more ephemeral of the poet's works. Also offers a peek into Espronceda's readings and literary preferences.

_____. *José de Espronceda et son temps. Littérature, société, politique au temps du romantisme*. Paris: Editious Klincksieck, 1974. An exhaustive, in-depth study of Espronceda, his times and his works (except for the later ones) by the author of the most recent editions of the poet. Suffers from the usual stylistic and organizational maladies attendant to a seven hundred plus page doctoral dissertation.

_____. «Lista et Espronceda. Fragments inédits du *Pelayo*. *Bulletin Hispanique*, 64 (1962), 526-37. Who did what in Espronceda's unfinished and undistinguished epic poem. Good source study.

MARTINENGO, ALESSANDRO. «Espronceda ante la leyenda faústica.»

Revista de Literatura, 57-58 (January-June 1966), 35-55. A recapitulation of the old theories concerning Espronceda's possible debts to Goethe's *Faust* plus the advancement of some new ones by this critic. One of the better articles on this topic.

NAVAS RUIZ, RICARDO. *El romanticismo español. Historia y crítica.* Salamanca: Anaya, 1970. Sketchy but complete, encyclopedia-like manual of Spanish Romanticism. Divided into chapters on genres and indiviudal authors. Includes very basic bibliographies.

PATTISON, WALTER T. «On Espronceda's Personality.» *Publications of the Modern Language Association,* 61 (1946), 1126-1145. An excellent essay not only on the poet's literary «personality,» but also a useful annotated chronology of the major poems. Perhaps the best, most concise and intelligent introduction to Espronceda and his poetry.

_____. «Sources of Espronceda's 'El Mendigo'.» In *Filología y Crítica Hispánica. Homenaje al Profesor Sánchez Escribano,* ed. Alberto Porqueras Mayo y Carlos Rojas. Emory University: Ediciones Alcalá, 1969, pp. 299-308. The discarding of previously suggested influences on one of Espronceda's best known poems and the advancing of new ones such as Izaak Walton's «Frank Davidson's Song» and Walter Scott's «Barefoot Friar» is thoroughly convincing.

PECKHAM, MORSE. «Toward a Theory of Romanticism.» *Publications of the Modern Language Association,* 66 (March 1951), 5-23. An intelligent and thorough discussion of the philosophical reasons behind the romantic movement which helps to understand the mind of the Romantics. Peckham reconsidered some of his earlier conclusions later in *Studies in Romanticism,* 1 (Autumn 1961), 1-8.

PEERS, EDGAR ALLISON. *A History of the Romantic Movement in Spain,* 2 volumes. Cambridge: The University Press, 1940. A complete survey of romantic literature in Spain. Done with great care and in minute detail. Remains useful if only for raw information such as dates, titles, etc. Its theses have been superseded, even if some still consider it the «standard» work.

_____. «Light Imagery in *El Estudiante de Salamanca.*» *Hispanic Review,* 9 (1941), 199-209. Interesting essay which charges light, color and darkness with emotional, circumstantial and implied meanings.

_____. «Studies in the Influence of Sir Walter Scott in Spain.» *Revue Hispanique,* 68 (1926), 1-160. Chapter II (pp. 40-69) of this long article is dedicated to Espronceda's *Sancho Saldaña.* Scott's *Ivanhoe, Quentin Durward, The Bride of Lammermoor,* and *The Fair Maid of Perth* are scrutinized as possible influences on the Spaniard's only novel.

PRAZ, MARIO. *The Romantic Agony.* London and New York: Oxford University Press, 1970. One of the basic and indispensable texts on Romanticism. Explores all of the tenents, some major figures and most of the symbolic meanings of romantic literature.

PUJALS, ESTEBAN. *Espronceda y Lord Byron,* 2nd edition. Madrid: Consejo Superior de Investigaciones Científicas, 1972. Examines in reasoned and careful detail the relationship and influences between the two poets. Extremely pertinent as a contrapuntal work to that of Philip H. Churchman.

SALINAS, PEDRO. «Espronceda. La rebelión contra la realidad.» In his *Ensayos de literatura hispánica.* Madrid: Aguilar, 1958, pp. 272-81. A philosophical and impressionistic discourse on Espronceda as the greatest poet to follow the two-hundred-year hiatus since Góngora and the Golden Age until nineteenth century Romanticism.

SAMUELS, DANIEL G. «Some Spanish Romantic Debts of Espronceda.» *Hispanic Review,* 16 (1948), 157-62. Leaving aside the usual Byron influences, Samuels looks at «A una estrella,» *Amor venga sus agravios* and *El Diablo Mundo* as works having an identifiable Spanish ascendancy.

SEBOLD, RUSSELL P. «El infernal arcano de Félix de Montemar.» *Hispanic Review,* 46 (Autumn 1978), 447-64. The hero of *El Estudiante de Salamanca* is seen not only as a womanizing, drinking, gambling and dueling Don Juan, but—more significantly—as a titanic Satan-like figure, challenger of God and the world order. A fine and important contribution.

SHAW, DONALD L. «Towards the Understanding of Spanish Romanticism.» *Modern Language Review*, 58 (April 1963), 190-95. A brief but fresh appraisal of the significance of Romanticism not only as a literary movement but as a cultural phenomenon. Reviews the earlier theories of Peers, Tarr and others.

TARR, F. COURTNEY. «Romanticism in Spain and Spanish Romanticism: A critical survey.» *Bulletin of Hispanic Studies*, 16 (1939), 3-37. One of the earliest and most perceptive essays differentiating between European Romanticism and its uniquely Spanish manifestations.

TORRES, ELÍAS. «García de Villalta y Espronceda. Un inmediato antecedente de 'El estudiante de Salamanca'.» *Insula,* 132 (November 1957), n.p. Interesting parallel between the two friends' works wherein both of their protagonists witness their own funerals.

Since García de Villalta's *El golpe en vago* was published in 1835, years earlier than *El estudiante de Salamanca,* Torres may have a point.

VASARI, STEPHEN. «'La pata de palo.' Fuente y sentido de un cuento de Espronceda.» *Papeles de Son Armadans,* 65 (1972), 49-56. The first and only study to date dedicated exclusively to this tale by Espronceda. Valuable for its bibliographical data and interesting in its interpretation of the story.

WARDROPPER, BRUCE. «Espronceda's 'Canto a Teresa' and the Spanish Elegiac Tradition.» *Bulletin of Hispanic Studies,* 45 (1963), 89-100. A historical and interpretative analysis of the poem. How Espronceda fits within the traditional poetic canons and therapeutic reasons he may have had for writing the Canto.

YNDURÁIN, DOMINGO. *Análisis formal de la poesía de Espronceda.* Madrid: Taurus, 1971. A formalistic approach to Espronceda's three narrative poems: *El Pelayo, El Estudiante de Salamanca* and *El Diablo Mundo*. Though replete with frequency counts and other statistical data, the work is inconclusive and of limited value.